HUNGER, TECHNOLOGY & LIMITS TO GROWTH

Christian Responsibility for Three Ethical Issues

ROBERT L. STIVERS

AUGSBURG Publishing House • Minneapolis

To my teachers in ethics:

John Bennett
Beverly Harrison
Reinhold Niebuhr
Roger Shinn
Ronald Stone

HUNGER, TECHNOLOGY, AND LIMITS TO GROWTH
Christian Responsibility for Three Ethical Issues

Copyright © 1984 Augsburg Publishing House

Scripture quotations unless otherwise noted are from the Revised Standard Version of the Bible, copyright 1946, 1952, and 1971 by the Division of Christian Education of the National Council of Churches.

Portions of Chapter 9, "Rigor and Responsibility," are reprinted by permission from the December 17, 1980 issue of *The Christian Century.* Copyright 1980 Christian Century Foundation.

Quotations from "The Power to Speak Truth to Power," the public policy statement on energy of the Presbyterian churches, are used by permission of the Stated Clerk of the General Assembly of the Presbyterian Church in the United States. Quotations from vols. I and II of *Faith and Science in an Unjust World* are used by permission of the World Council of Churches.

Library of Congress Cataloging in Publication Data

Stivers, Robert L., 1940-
   HUNGER, TECHNOLOGY & LIMITS TO GROWTH.

   1. Church and the poor. 2. Technology—Religious aspects—Christianity. 3. Human ecology—Religious aspects—Christianity. I. Title.
BV639.P6S75 1984   261.8   83-72120
ISBN 0-8066-2064-1

Manufactured in the U.S.A.   APH 10-3184
1 2 3 4 5 6 7 8 9 0 1 2 3 4 5 6 7 8 9

CONTENTS

69/96

PREFACE

I teach Christian ethics at a private liberal arts college. Teaching Christian ethics at the college level is not a particularly hazardous or unpleasant undertaking. Occupational satisfaction for college professors is the highest of all professional groups. While the pay is not high in comparison to other professions, the intangibles in terms of personal freedom, interaction with people, and the general environment are difficult to match. All in all, college professors are a privileged group and have no reason to complain.

Nevertheless teaching, in particular teaching ethics, has its hazards. The worst comes from being a normal human being with average vices when many expect an ethical superstar. In part this hazard is self-inflicted and a problem for anyone who lives consciously in the gray area between who they are in their average moments and who they might be if the Holy Spirit possessed them totally.

In most jobs or professions the tension between who you are and who you might or should be is not so acute. This is not to say ethical standards are nonexistent in other jobs or professions. Each has its set of standards. In most cases, however, the standards are not so exacting nor the deviations so intolerable as in the profession of teaching ethics, which seeks to explore the standards for standards and to occupy itself full time with the ideal and deviations from the ideal. Having such subjects continually in mind draws attention to things that would be more conveniently shipped off into some shadowy recess.

Teaching young adults on the college level brings exposure to an unusually high number of idealists and heightens the tension. Teaching older adults wizened by the necessities and inevitability of compromise is far easier. Students are a thorn in the side, continually pricking open the wounds of compromise. With no possessions, little or no family responsibility, and few skeletons in the closet, it is easy for them to pick up the cross of radical idealism and to use it as a cudgel on hypocrisy.

As long as it is not my hypocrisy they expose, I admire the students for this. In particular, I admired myself as a student. I had a keen sense of how much middle-aged professors deviated from my ideals and hence lacked my moral virtue. Now that I have found the log in my own eye—just in time, as it were, to allow for the convenient compromise of my present affluence—I can speak back to my students about the slivers in their eyes. How easy it is to use the study of ethics to defend the peccadillos of the present and to assault the defenses of your critics! All sorts of flip-flops make sense, and teachers of ethics turn into magicians.

In a more serious vein, students do have a crucial role to play in ethics. Unburdened, the morally sensitive student serves as a standard bearer for rigor, truth, and beauty. Without such students everyone would be impoverished, for the compromise of ethical standards would be all the easier.

This volume is about my own affluence, rigor, and compromise and that of many Americans, for I am not alone. I have been goaded into writing by my students and by several moral perfectionists, none of whom have let me get away easily with my compromises. The primary motif is struggle. This is not a finished product with final ethical pronouncements but a book which talks about beginning. It is my struggle, but also the struggle of affluent American Christians with the rigor of the Christian ethic as it applies to the problems of world poverty, alienation in a technological society, and shortages of energy and resources.

In this struggle there is a dilemma which can be stated succinctly. It is the dilemma of prosperity. On the one hand, I am troubled by my own prosperity: it sticks out like a sore thumb in a world of poor people, it contributes to a host of modern problems, and it may not be sustainable. On the other hand, I appreciate and enjoy my prosperity and want it to continue.

I prefer vehicles which are miserly when it comes to fuel, but I appreciate the mobility of cars and planes. I prefer small, closely knit communities, but I also like a house with room to get away and appliances that eliminate the drudgery. Affluence and consumption are not bad words with me, but by the same token poverty, alienation, and unsustainability are not good words. I am troubled and have doubts whether I can have my cake and eat it too.

To expand and overdo it a bit, I can imagine my material delights in a struggle with five foes. The first foe is the ethics of the kingdom of God as stated, for example, in the Sermon on the Mount. Several questions suggest the nature of the struggle. Does the ethical rigor of the kingdom ethic represent the only valid Christian option? Is this ethic incumbent on all Christians, and, if so, are compromises acceptable? Is it possible to live anything but a life of self-denial if this ethic is taken seriously? How can we realistically live this ethic in a world of wolves and serpents?

The second foe of my affluence and consumption is the poor and hungry of the world. Can I, in good conscience, consume as heavily as I do, while so many others are crying out for the very things which I take for granted as ordinary and necessary consumption? Does my level of consumption square even with the rigorous call of Jesus to be just and to love my neighbor as myself? And what if I did lower my consumption? Would this do anything concrete for the poor and hungry?

The third foe is the dispiriting and nonparticipatory nature of modern technological society. Here ambiguity is especially prevalent. On the one hand, I hear and experience the teachings of Jesus about possessions plugging my ears to the hearing of God's Word. On the other hand, I know how possessions and the consumption of energy and resources make possible creative experiences where the Word is heard in a new way. Is it possible, short of self-denial, to avoid the spirit-numbing nature of material consumption? In what way does my consumption help to perpetuate a system which tends increasingly to be large and impersonal and to provide fewer opportunities for citizen participation? Put differently, does not my consumption signal a desire for the perpetuation of these trends and for the legitimation of only seeking "technical fixes" to current problems?

The fourth foe is sustainability. Here the questions revolve around the legacy I and people like me are leaving to future generations. Most observers now concede that American levels of resource and energy consumption, if adopted worldwide, would not be sustainable very long. There is even serious question whether these levels are sustainable even for the few of us who enjoy them now. How long such levels are can be sustained and at what levels depends on technological breakthroughs and value changes which are difficult to forecast. The tough question is whether my present consumption will leave an impoverishing legacy. In Christian terms, the question is about the meaning of stewardship. What does it mean to be a good steward of energy and resources at this time? Does it mean major cutbacks, minor alterations, or business as usual?

The fifth foe is the difficulty and slow pace of social change. I am convinced that individual life-style alterations and appeals to voluntarism, however important, will not produce the change required by the challenge of poverty, alienation, and sustainability. My struggle here is a classic one. If I cut back the things I enjoy while the majority proceed as usual, I may feel righteous but will have done little to grapple with the problem. My reduced demand, in fact, makes it possible for others to consume more. The question then becomes how best to bring about laws and social actions that will deal with the communal nature of the problems. On the personal level, the struggle is over the budgeting of limited personal energy, a struggle between the comforts of affluence and consumption on the one side and the hard work and the frustrations of social action on the other. Some nights it's just easier to sit in front of the fire than it is to mount the energy to go out and attend still another community action committee meeting.

These are my struggles. They do not permit detachment, at least not for me. Worst of all they persist, for most of my questions do not have conclusive answers or deal with the unpredictable future. As a consequence, this is, I must repeat, an unfinished book and the suggestions for change I make in what follows are all tentative. It would be nice if modern social problems and appropriate Christian responses could be stated in simple terms. As a student of a few of these problems, I wish I could go further and offer simple, quick, and workable solutions. I wish finally that I could cut through the swamp of moral relativity and offer the one and only Christian way.

These are wishes I cannot deliver, and I am suspicious of anyone who makes facile diagnoses and offers easy ways out. Complexity and relativity are givens. They will not pass away with the wave of some magic wand. The trick, I am convinced, is to develop an appreciation of complexity and relativity without becoming immobilized.

To conclude this personal beginning, some indication of why I have taken the trouble to be so personal is in order. The first reason comes from an understanding of how ethical perceptions are formed. For most people, ethical perceptions are primarily a product of social forces and a limited amount of freedom. Of considerable importance in evaluating a person's ethical conclusions is knowledge of his or her background, occupation, and problems. By revealing a bit about myself at the outset, I am not trying to be narcissistic but wish to provide the reader with a basis for evaluating what follows. That I am a professor and not a businessman is important to the way I see things. That I have a Christian background will mean I have certain biases. That I am troubled by certain problems and not by others may or may not provide a point of contact.

This leads to the second reason. I am convinced I am not alone in the things that trouble me. Some are troubled more, some less than I about these things; but perhaps if I, who have the time and inclination to write, am able to struggle some, then others might be helped through the gates I have opened. This is my hope.

Several people have helped me in my writing and I am grateful. The officers of Pacific Lutheran University have been generous in their support. My colleagues have suffered through various drafts. Two assistants, Debbie Florian and Bev Tschimperle, typed and retyped several of the chapters. My wife Sylvia and children Laura and Mark kept me going. I am also grateful to the United Presbyterian Church in the U.S.A. and the Presbyterian Church in the U.S., especially Dean Lewis and Gaspar Langella, for the chance to work out several ideas in a joint task force of these denominations and to attend the World Council of Churches conference at M.I.T. Finally, I thank the *Christian Century* for permission to use parts of an essay, "Deciding on Christian Lifestyles," which first appeared in the December 17, 1980 issue.

PART 1

Putting on the Brakes

CHAPTER 1

Forks in the Road

Being an American Christian today is like riding in a car that has come to an unsignaled end in a stretch of the Interstate Highway System. Only minutes before everything seemed normal. Nothing indicated the changes that were about to occur, or at least nothing we were aware of at high speeds of travel. The road was smooth, the way well marked. The landscaping was a little brown from the exhaust of so many vehicles but still appealing to the eye. The eight-cylinder engine was running smoothly, fueled by a recently filled 20-gallon tank of inexpensive gasoline. It was an effort just to keep the speed down to 70 miles per hour. Everything seemed to conspire for a faster rate of "progress."

To say the superhighway has come to an unsignaled end is not entirely accurate. The speed limit signs have been repainted to read 55 instead of 65 or 70, but the change has been largely ignored. And the way does go on. In fact the road is even acceptable for awhile, but six lanes become four and then two. The pavement changes to gravel and then to dirt. The way is unmarked, and up ahead, warns a friendly passerby, are a series of forks which will require us to make choices for which we have very little preparation.

This analogy of a deteriorating road system is not meant as a prediction. Americans may indeed face the prospect of crumbling superhighways and reduced standards of material living. Such an eventuality is only one of the possibilities, however. Just as likely is a society which puts its full energies into modern technology to avoid production and consumption limits, or even a society which elects to pursue other less economically oriented ends such as leisure, conversation, and art.

This analogy is meant rather to suggest different ways of thinking about basic assumptions and about who American Christians are and what they are doing. The wide, easy way of economic growth, technical progress, and heavy consumption of material goods has come into serious question. Things that were passed at high speed yesterday are now causing us to take a second look. The road to the future is not quite so open and smooth, at least not as Americans consider the implications of present directions.

Three Major Problems

Three major problems have put the brakes on assumptions and actions regarding economic growth, technical progress, and material consumption previously taken for granted. The first is an old problem which has been acting as a partial brake for some time. In simplest terms, it has to do with social justice and pits American affluence against the poverty and malnourishment of the world's poor.

The problem is not so much that Americans are rich and so many others are poor. After all, Americans did work hard to produce their system of abundance, and transferring wealth to the poor is more difficult than most imagine. The failure is rather a moral one. Injustice comes from failure to look closely at the landscape alongside the superhighway, a failure to share and to see the side effects of high-speed driving such as the often unfair terms of trade, the inordinate influence of large American organizations pursuing their own interests, and the support given to repressive rulers and local elites. The fact is that the consumption of Americans and the activities of its corporate, governmental, and even religious representatives contribute, sometimes substantially, to the injustice and lack of power which are the root causes of poverty and malnutrition. This injustice is exacerbated by the failure of Americans to give types of assistance which reach the poor and amounts which can make a dent in the incidence of poverty. Studies on nonmilitary foreign aid repeatedly paint a different picture than that of a generous and caring nation.

The second problem, while hardly new, has been felt with increasing intensity as the size and impersonality of modern social structures have increased. In the United States the issue is the frustration, powerlessness, and alienation that many feel in dealing with these structures. The pressures on the family, the widespread notion that technology is out of control, the lack of close-knit communities, and a decreasing sense of participation all point to the problem. In developing countries the problem is the breaking up of traditional communities due to the introduction of new economic policies, the domination of social structures by foreign interests and a small collaborating elite, and the compelling quality of mass consumption. For want of a better term, this potpourri of issues may be called the problem of participation, for one of its root causes is a lack of sharing in decisions made at higher levels or by impersonal market forces.

The third problem is more recent in origin. Negatively, it is called limits to growth, and positively, the problem of long-range sustainability. Along with rising fuel costs and a new awareness about pollution, it has done more than anything else to raise questions about the basic assumptions and actions of Americans. To some it is a pseudo-problem. To others, however, it represents a real threat to plans for the elimination of poverty and malnutrition. Simply stated, the problem involves limits in five areas which are now experiencing growth: 1) food, 2) population, 3) energy, 4) natural resources, and 5) pollution. Several questions are now being asked about growth. How long and at what levels can expansion in each of these areas be sustained? Are there limits to expansion or does the technological process offer a future of unlimited abundance? How are the problems interrelated? Finally, are there social limits to our ability to solve these problems?

The Just, Participatory, and Sustainable Society

Each of these problems deserves and will receive further attention. What is important at this stage is to see that Christians differ in their perceptions of these problems and have different options available for dealing with them. In the United States, sustainability is perceived as the major problem and options range from technological "fixes" to changed life-styles to withdrawal from the larger society. Christians living in poorer countries perceive justice and participation as the major problems. They have far fewer options, and in some cases none at all. But they do have one major advantage, if it can be called such. Many of them are already living sustainable lives, that is, sustainable and poverty-stricken. These and other differences between Christians in various parts of the world are significant and must be understood by American Christians if they are to make responsible choices.

The Christian forum where these problems have received their most open airing is the World Council of Churches. Since 1966 the World Council has concentrated a good deal of its energies on hearing and responding to the voices of the world's poor. During the 1970s, the Council's section on church and society undertook a series of international conferences dealing with faith, science, and the future.[1] From these conferences emerged an ecumenical vision of a future society which was awkwardly but accurately called the *just, participatory, and sustainable society.*

The reasons for the awkwardness of the title are largely historical and reflect the diversity of the discussions. In the first years of the Council's new concentration on the world's poor, discussions centered on social justice and, to a lesser degree, participation. Economic and technological growth were assumed to be both beneficial and unlimited. Early in the 1970s doubts about these assumptions began to be heard. An even newer emphasis appeared which questioned the sustainability of present patterns of economic and technological growth and pointed to the many unintended side effects of new technologies. This newer emphasis, because it threatened several important initiatives, startled, confused, and in some instances antagonized Christians who had been working for social justice. The conferences subsequent to the introduction of this newer emphasis, including a large gathering at the Massachusetts Institute of Technology in the summer of 1979, wrestled with the relation of justice, participation, and sustainability to each other and insisted on placing each in the title while relationships and priorities were worked out.

The ecumenical vision of the just, participatory, and sustainable society which has emerged from these conferences is far from a blueprint. To the contrary, the vision in these conferences served more as a catalyst, a vague and problematic image intended to start discussion, to give order to old concerns, and to open up new horizons.

The first of the conferences to use the word *sustainable* was a 1974 gathering in Bucharest, Romania. The conference report had this to say by way of introduction to what it called the "long-term concept of a sustainable and just society":

> Feeling a responsibility at least for our grandchildren, and sensing an incapacity for the environment to support for long a load significantly higher than today's, we believe that the rich segments of the world have now reached the critical point where material expansion will reduce the quality of life for some people at some time within the period of concern to us. The remaining, poorer members of humanity are at a stage where the current benefits of material expansion, except in terms of population, are far larger than the probable costs in terms of reduced quality of life now or in the relevant future. Thus today the worldwide quality of life will be increased by material growth among the poor and by stabilization and possibly contraction among the rich.

As for content, the Bucharest report went on to delineate a few characteristics of its vision of the future.

> First, social stability cannot be obtained without an equitable distribution of what is in scarce supply or without common opportunity to participate in social decisions. Second, a robust global society will not be sustained unless the need for food is at any time well below capacity to supply it, and unless the emissions of pollutants are well below the capacity of the ecosystem to absorb them. Third, the new social organization will be sustainable only as long as the rate of use of nonrenewable resources does not outrun the increase in resources made available through technological innovation. Finally, a sustainable society requires a level of human activity which is not adversely influenced by the never ending, large and frequent natural variation in global climate.

> In essence, the sustainable society will be one with a stable population and with a fixed material wealth per person, a so-

ciety actively pursuing quality of life in basically nonmaterial
dimensions such as leisure, service, arts, education and sport.
. . . More concretely, we foresee a world where (1) the security
of the individual, (2) the redistribution of material wealth,
and (3) the implementation of a maximum consumption level
are all affected by a transnational social security system divid-
ing the responsibility for the fate of the individual among all
people.[2]

The conferences which followed spelled this out in greater
detail,[3] but for the most part avoided any comprehensive plan.
There seemed to be an unstated preference to let discussions
range around a number of topics from energy to bioethics, to
a new economic order, to an underlying theological stance, all
of which related to the main theme.

What then is the just, participatory, and sustainable society?
To answer this question it is necessary to supplement the Council's discussions with the increasing body of literature on the
topic.[4] In summary, the just, participatory, and sustainable society is a vision of a new world society with three major components: 1) an economic order, 2) a political system, and 3) an
ethic or world view.

The new economic order is clear in broad outline but vague
in particulars. Its goals would be 1) the provision of basic human
needs such as food, housing, clothing, and some margin above
subsistence, this margin depending on what can be sustained
over the long haul; 2) the reduction of inequalities in wealth,
income, and power; 3) indefinite sustainability with regard to
population and the consumption of energy and resources; and 4)
environmental soundness. Such an economic system would be in
equilibrium with basic ecological support systems and would
minimize, not maximize, the consumption of nonrenewable resources. Growth would not be eliminated. The growth of non-
polluting, nondepleting forms of economic activity would go on
and be encouraged. Durability, recycling, and the elimination of
waste would be high priorities. Local self-reliance and participation in the what and how of production decisions would,
within reason, be an important consideration since dependency
and nonparticipation have been shown to be unproductive.[5]
New technologies would also be encouraged but, unlike now,
would be carefully tailored to the goals and to local needs. Particular attention would be given to so-called soft [6] or appro-

priate [7] technologies, that is, technologies which are less energy
and resource intensive and tailored to local needs and end use.
The political system, while crucial, is also problematic. The
basics are clear enough. Beyond the normal functions of political units—often overwhelming in themselves and not easily gone
beyond—the new political system would have to manage worldwide sustainability, reduce inequalities, work toward local self-
reliance and participation, and find alternatives to the arms
race and war. Whether this is beyond human capacity remains
to be seen, but that it is a gargantuan challenge few will deny.
What kind of political structures could meet such a challenge?
Some form of centralized power would be required to manage
sustainability and conflict and to maintain a rough equality, but
excessive centralization would probably be devastating to participation and local community. The reverse problem would per-
tain to decentralized structures.

These political difficulties could be markedly reduced if a new
ethic or world view with changed attitudes and values emerged.
Describing and making a case for this new world view is the
principal objective of this volume. Several things can be said
about it. First, for Christians at least, the world view must be
based on biblically derived assumptions and values. Second, it
must modify many current assumptions and values, especially
those which have contributed to the three problems stated in
the preceding section. Of particular importance here will be an
emphasis on the three norms of justice, participation, and, as
we will later call it, sustainable sufficiency. This includes the
recognition that justice and participation without sustainable
sufficiency are impossible and sustainable sufficiency without
justice and participation is morally out of the question.

Third, certain Christian insights will be of special value to
this world view. Among the most important are the Christian
understanding of sin and its relation to limits; the Christian concern for the poor, for social justice, and for liberation; the call
of Jesus Christ and the apostle Paul to sharing and their warnings about the dangers of wealth and possessions; the early
Christian emphasis on small, holistic communities; the Christian
notion of stewardship, meaning care for persons and nature;
central theological understandings such as the kingdom of God,
the cross and resurrection, and life between the ages; and finally
the examples of Jesus and Paul. From these sources can be drawn

a fairly coherent world view or ethic which gives foundation to the necessary political and economic structures.

The Debate Over Sustainability and Vision

The flavor of the World Council discussions and the differences which arose were evident in the 1979 conference at the Massachusetts Institute of Technology. Early in the program Dr. C. T. Kurien, economist, director of the Madras Institute of Developmental Studies, and a representative of the Church of South India, launched a blistering attack on the concept of sustainability and on naive and innocent visionaries who design utopian fantasies empty of significant content.[8]

Dr. Kurien's attack on sustainability was not motivated by ignorance about economic and technological growth in a finite world. What bothered him was the way in which the concept was being used to protect the already affluent. Persistently he put the questions: sustainability—how, where, and for whom? In Kurien's eyes the popularity of the concept can be attributed to two things: 1) the pseudo-scientific propaganda by which it is being sold and 2) the anxiety of a pampered minority about its affluence and wasteful way of life. Basically, he claimed, sustainability is a problem only for this pampered minority whose economic systems—be they capitalist or communist—demand ever-greater expansion. Their problem is protecting themselves and their extravagant way of life. They are proclaiming a noble concept on behalf of the world's poor and future generations to disguise a problem of their own making. Paraphrasing John in the New Testament he went on to say:

> If you claim to be concerned about the unborn humanity that you cannot see, but show no regard for the humanity that you can see all around you, then you are a liar. It is a small affluent minority of the world's population that whips up a hysteria about the finite resources of the world and pleads for a conservationist ethic in the interests of those yet to be born; it is the same group that makes an organized effort to prevent those who now happen to be outside the gates of their affluence from coming to have even a tolerable level of living. It does not call for a divine's insight to see what the real intentions are.[9]

For the vast majority in poorer countries, argued Kurien, sustainability is not a problem. When all the energy runs out the poor will survive, for in large measure they are already living in traditionally sustainable ways. Given the truth of this, Kurien then asked, "In whose name are we conducting our 'sustainable society' discussions?"

As for the question of how, Kurien had little patience for visions of the future that do not concretely spell out the "how." "I don't believe," he went on to say, "in any prescription about 'growth' . . . which does not also spell out the social processes that will make that prescription operational . . . (W)ords like 'growth' and 'sustainable society' are empty, though emotive, and . . . therefore one cannot discuss them effectively unless one puts content into them."

Later, the working group in which Kurien participated presented a report, after sharp debate, which largely submerged the concept of sustainability under justice and participation, stating in one place that sustainability is a "condition of justice."[10] Within the group sides were drawn more or less along north/ south lines, with those from the affluent north holding out for sustainability as a separate and distinct concept, concrete details notwithstanding. While acknowledging the concerns of Kurien and others, they argued the need for visions of the future, in particular the vision of the just, participatory, and sustainable society. On the one hand, they admitted the absence of concrete details might betray naiveté, ideological bias, and anxieties about affluence. Certainly those dangers are ever present and must be guarded against. On the other hand, especially in developed countries, the concept of sustainability is closely related to justice, participation, and visions of the future essential for the setting of new directions.

A few within the group forcibly put the case for sustainability as a concept coequal with justice and participation in the World Council's vision of the future. They argued that limits to economic expansion, be they physical or social, are with us whether or not justice and participation are considered. Granted they are more of a problem for the rich, but just the same they affect persons in all countries. Because one lives off the land in traditionally sustainable fashion does not guarantee immunity from the consequences of limits.

Others pointed out that the awareness of limits and of the

need for more sustainable modes was an important conceptual
tool to raise questions about the assumptions of the affluent.
Contrary to Kurien's emphasis on sustainability as an ideological dodge, they maintained that the concept, when coupled with
the notion of sufficiency, provides an opportunity to change
wasteful and excessive consumption patterns which contribute
to the injustice and lack of participation in poorer countries.
Their position rested, of course, on the assumption that changed
awareness leads to changed patterns of consumption. It is an
assumption Dr. Kurien did not respond to but might reject for
its failure to deal with structures in social change, that is, the
failure to attend to the "how" question.

Still others argued that Dr. Kurien was prematurely cutting
off a very significant discussion. That the concepts of justice,
participation, and sustainability lack specific content in World
Council deliberations is not sufficient reason to cut off the discussion. Further deliberation might produce the needed content
and clarify the relation between the concepts in a way which
would help both rich and poor to attain higher levels of justice
and participation. Nor, they added, is the World Council alone
in thinking about these issues. A growing body of literature
about sustainability is available to go along with the considerable materials on justice and participation. The "how" question
really is not that empty of content.

Finally some spoke of the importance of future visions, rejecting Kurien's charges of innocence and naiveté. Their concern was to find an alternative to the technological vision of the
day, which sees things in narrow terms of efficiency, production,
and scientific rationality. Perhaps the technological vision is not
a problem in Third World countries, they rejoined, but it is a
powerful vision which has swallowed up traditional western
ways of thinking and doing and is already causing changes in
many poor countries. In any case, there is a problem of participation and lack of alternative visions in the developed countries
which the vision of the just, participatory, and sustainable society
addresses. Sustainability is very important in this mix, for it
exposes the negative side effects of the technological vision.

Visions of the future are critical in their own right, they went
on to say, and are sometimes most effective when not filled with
detailed content. Visions enliven the present and give it meaning
and direction. They are vehicles, however limited, of social

change. "Without vision," as Proverbs tells us, "the people perish" (Prov. 29:18 KJV).

That there is a need for new visions is not sufficient in itself, of course, to produce a coherent and effective vision. Here Dr. Kurien was on the right track. Effective visions of the future cannot be produced out of whole cloth by a discussion group or at the stroke of a dissatisfied academic's pen. According to French sociologist Jacques Ellul, three factors must be present. Visions of the future must emerge from the real experiences of a people, must be potentially realizable, and must reflect at least some of the values held in common by the people. Ellul warns:

> If all three factors are not present, or if the second and third are lacking, no invented concept of the future could possibly be implemented. None would possess the power to put the social body into motion, give it meaning and direction—a "raison de vivre." For an image of the future to have some real value, it must appear capable of being lived, not merely desired—not only by individuals who believe it but by the social body as a whole.
>
> We must energetically reject the irresponsible attitude that says: "We don't know what is really efficacious. Let us dream up any image of the future that appeals to us; let us throw the bottle into the sea; it may reach land somewhere. An idea seemingly devoid of all consequence eventually will have, perhaps only after centuries, immense repercussions; therefore, let us not bother with real consequences but rather hold to our dreams and desires." [11]

For Dr. Kurien, the just, participatory, and sustainable society fails to meet these criteria with regard to sustainability. Sustainability is not the concern of the poor. It is not realizable in developed countries unless more specific content is provided. Most of all it reflects the values and anxieties of the rich and is thus largely irrelevant to the context of the poor. Justice and participation are different, according to Kurien, for they grow out of the lived experience of poor people, are their genuine aspirations, and have been shown in many instances to be realizable and to improve conditions.

The disagreement in part reflects differences of context. While Dr. Kurien may be correct with regard to the poor, he does not necessarily speak to the context of the rich. The threat of limits and the need for change to forms of consumption which are both sufficient and sustainable are very real in countries like the United States. Sustainability will be a necessary criterion eventually; only the length of the transition and the levels of output consistent with long-range sustainability remain in doubt. The only criterion not satisfied is the third. Sustainability is foreign to American ways of thinking and doing. But even here economic necessity may eventually influence values. An effective vision which couples sustainable sufficiency with justice and participation may hasten the process and help to arrive at a democratic and equitable outcome.

Several things may be concluded from this debate. Among Christians real differences exist reflecting diversity of location in a stratified, unequal, and disunited world. These differences must be acknowledged and attempts made to keep the dialog going. American Christians, for their part, need to take Dr. Kurien seriously and go out of their way to avoid letting sustainability become a disguise for the status quo or the slogan of reactionary groups. They also need to work on the content—scientific, political, and theological—of any visions which include sustainability. Dr. Kurien and those who acknowledge him as a spokesperson should in turn recognize that the concept of sustainability is important in certain contexts, at the same time that they keep pressure on those who use it. The concept of sustainability itself should be retained alongside justice and participation in the World Council discussions. The problem it points to is serious, whether or not it is perceived so in all quarters, and the concept is relevant to problems which are not confined just to developed countries.

In regard to visions of the future, Dr. Kurien's criticisms should be taken as warnings and attention paid to Jacques Ellul's criteria. The just, participatory, and sustainable society must be seen as a tentative vision, not as something coextensive with the kingdom of God, but a working idea for which content must be provided.

This last conclusion calls for an additional note about visions and their relation to the work of God through the Holy Spirit. For sociologist Elise Boulding, effective visions of the future must have both transcendent and human dimensions.[12] From a Christian perspective this means that visions like the just, participatory, and sustainable society, while acknowledged to be works of the imagination, need to be grounded in the work of the Spirit. The transcendent dimension provides the necessary base to break the bonds of current thinking and doing and to overcome the impasse of relativity. The human dimension is equally necessary. Not only is the Holy Spirit present in the thoughts and actions of individuals and groups, but effective visions, as Ellul has pointed out, must emerge from the experience, values, and aspirations of living people. In effect Boulding is saying that Christians should see themselves as co-creators with God, free to construct tentative visions of the future and to work diligently for them, yet dependent on the Spirit for the energy to persevere, the openness to respond, and the power for self-criticism.

The relation of visions like the just, participatory, and sustainable society to the kingdom of God must be seen in this light. This vision is not to be confused with the kingdom because it is a work of the imagination. All such works fall short of the kingdom which God alone will bring in to complete what was begun in Jesus Christ. Nevertheless, this vision does participate in the reality of the kingdom, however tentatively. Justice, participative communities, and careful stewardship are the work of God and have been from the very start. This vision also represents the self-conscious efforts of Christians trying to figure out what it means to be a follower of Jesus Christ in the present day. Christians need these visionary embodiments of the kingdom of God to give direction, but they also need to keep in mind continually that the real source of visions is God who is also the judge of human thinking and doing.

It is in this spirit that the work of the World Council goes on.

It must be emphasized that within the ecumenical movement we are far from reaching any measure of consensus about the role of science and technology in achieving the just, participatory, and sustainable society, and for good reason. The churches have themselves only truly begun their enquiries and for some time to come there are bound to be wide differences of opinion on these issues. . . .

The ethical dilemmas and choices raised in relation to the idea of a sustainable society are truly immense. . . .

When today we enter into the discussion of the just and sustainable society, we must therefore have no illusions that we can "solve" any of these problems.[13]

Choices

"The predicament of the prosperous" is the term Larry Rasmussen and Bruce Birch use to describe the challenge of justice,
participation, and sustainable sufficiency to most Americans.[14]
Part of the predicament is that American Christians can no
longer rely on their superhighway assumptions about the economic and technological process to guide them to the goal of an
abundant and just future. The road they are now on may once
again find its way back to these assumptions and put them on a
superhighway at high speeds, but this is doubtful any time soon.
For now there is a different problem, negotiating a series of forks
in the road which lie just beyond the end of their superhighway
assumptions.

The three forks represent a series of choices confronting American Christians. The challenge for them is to select that choice
which is the most appropriate Christian response to the three
problems summarized earlier and which gets them on the road
to the just, participatory, and sustainable society, whether that
road is eventually a superhighway, merely a hardsurface, or a
wagon track. None of the choices by itself can be claimed as the
only appropriate Christian response, although Christians will
be found at each fork stoutly maintaining their preferences. The
basic questions at each fork are which road leads to the just,
participatory, and sustainable society and is it a road which individuals and groups can negotiate. Some may still want to ask
only for the quickest way back to the superhighway. But American Christians should not be in too much of a hurry, for it was
the superhighway which brought them to these forks in the first
place.

To the right at the first fork stand the so-called technological
optimists, barking pleas for freedom to apply their genies to the
problem of production. This road, the optimists claim, involves
no change in basic assumptions and is the fastest way back to
the superhighway from which it is just a short way to the just,
participatory, and sustainable society. Sustainable sufficiency is
a matter of production and a problem only to those who lack
imagination. As for justice and participation, they will trickle
down once abundance produces the leisure to develop appropriate structures. This road is attractive because it looks familiar
and requires no changes. But the attractiveness may also be

deceptive as American Christians consider the problem of participation and the role technology has played in bringing them to this fork.

The left-hand road is not familiar. Its visitors information center has a sign outside reading "The Road of Change." Inside the center are a number of brochures offering a wide range of options, from insulating houses and organic farming to space colonies and solar electric farms.

The choice is difficult. For reasons of prudence in the face of possible limits, of concern for the side effects of many new technologies, and of doubt about the trickle-down theory of helping the poor, many Christians turn left. In so doing they do not reject science-based technology. They merely want to make sure it remains a means and does not become an end in itself.

But having made this decision, they are immediately confronted by another fork. To the right at this fork is a sign whose headline reads "The Road of Technical and Structural Change." The fine print goes on to reveal that the way to justice, participation, and sustainable sufficiency is through changed industrial technologies and social engineering. Once societies plan the future and construct social institutions which maximize altruism, then justice, participation, and sustainable sufficiency will follow automatically.

Attracted by the seeming simplicity of this alternative, Christians are troubled by three critical assumptions that are nowhere made clear on the sign. The first assumption is that good institutions make good people, an assumption which, depending on how steadfastly it is maintained, may contradict the Christian understanding of sin. The second is that technology and social engineering are the keys to social change. This assumption may be partially correct, especially in modern industrial countries, but as a total explanation of change it overlooks the role of values and beliefs. Finally, there is an assumption about the effectiveness of planning and social engineering. Yes, humans have the freedom to change structures, but everywhere this freedom is limited by the staying power of inherited institutions and countered by another freedom, the freedom to unmake what has been made. Only a tyrannical form of planning could overcome the present disunity of the human race. And who is to trust the planners who often seem as confused and as subject to political manipulation as anyone else?

The road to the left, however, may be too unfamiliar. The headline on the sign reads, "The Road of Major Change in Values and Ways of Living." The fine print briefly indicates that changes are necessary, not just in planning and technology, but also in the way Americans live as individuals, the way they organize their social life, and the way they respond to the gospel of Jesus Christ. There seems to be an underlying mood that change must occur across the broad range of factors—economic, political, technical, and ethical—that make up complex societies.

The number of Christians who take the road of major change is smaller, but they are of nearly unanimous opinion that the situation calls for more than social and technical engineering. The road to justice, participation, and sustainable sufficiency must, they believe, include a reevaluation of who they are and the way they live. Whizzing past these things at 70 miles per hour will no longer suffice.

But again, having made this choice and taken the appropriate road, they immediately come to a third, and for some the most troubling, fork. On the one hand stands a woman holding a sign reading "Responsible Consumption." Asked what she means by her sign, she responds by saying that responsible consumption is a Christian option which takes the three problems and their world context seriously while avoiding the extreme of self-denial. It is a choice which wrestles with the dilemma of relating the ideal of the kingdom of God to the realities of everyday life. Taking this road involves flexibility, a living between the old age of sin and death and the new age of life in Christ. Several things are called for: in response to injustice, poverty, and mal-nutrition—sharing and advocacy; in response to centralized and exploitive social structures—new ways of being and doing which improve participation and community; in response to sustainable sufficiency—conservation, reduced personal and social consumption of certain things, and concentration on renewable sources of energy. The woman goes on to explain that the problem is not so much perfection or radical obedience, but how to act responsibly and begin a process of change which will lead to greater justice and participation and to a pattern of sustainable consumption. This process need not lead to a life of austerity and poverty unless that is a personal choice.

On the other hand is a young man enthusiastically proclaiming the virtues of the more rigorous road of total discipleship and solidarity with the poor. His sign reads, "Rigorous Discipleship." His response to questions is simpler and more direct. In the present situation, being a Christian and taking this road means such things as cutting back to a level of consumption which satisfies only basic needs, the building of and living in new communities of love, and the giving of what one has to the poor. In short, it means radical change and involves a total commitment to the kingdom of God which has been inaugurated by Jesus Christ and is present through the work of the Holy Spirit.

The issue for what follows is joined. Is it consistent with the life and work of Jesus Christ to be "reasonably" comfortable in an age of widespread poverty, malnutrition, advanced materialism, and limits to certain forms of growth? Is living in "reasonable" comfort under such conditions a cop-out, with the only faithful response being obedience to the radical claims of the ethics of the kingdom?

But while the issue is joined and some are ready to make their choices, time to reflect is needed. American Christians must pitch their tents or park their campers at this fork and consider the choices more carefully. They must investigate the three problems in greater detail, take a look at biblical and theological resources, and refine the options.

CHAPTER 2

Poverty and Malnutrition

Justice, participation, and sustainable sufficiency are the three problems the World Council of Churches is asking Christians to address. The first step is to get acquainted with the problems. In this chapter the problem is justice, more specifically the problem of injustice in the form of poverty and malnutrition. It is the first problem to be considered, not only because C. T. Kurien and others so insist, but because it is the most immediate of the three.

By conservative estimate 700 million people are malnourished throughout the world. Almost all of these people are poor. Most live outside the United States under conditions most Americans would find hard to believe. Some live within the United States even though the worst ravages of hunger and poverty have nearly been eliminated through economic expansion and a variety of social programs. But even with these efforts, in 1981 approximately 14% of Americans lived below the officially established poverty level of $9,287 for a family of four, and their number is growing as inflation and unemployment take their toll.[1] Fourteen percent is approximately 32 million people, and $9,287 for a family of four does not even cover the basics. Many of these people are hard to find, hidden in back of bolted doors in the slums of big cities, behind a row of trees in a migrant camp, among the hills of Appalachia, or on the vast plains of the West. They are forceful reminders that not all Americans are driving on the superhighway of abundance.

By comparison to the really poor of the world, most of America's poor are well off, at least in terms of statistical measures. The number and percentage of malnourished and poor people in developing countries is staggering. According to the Internation Labor Organization (ILO), 1.25 billion people are seriously poor and 700 million destitute.[2] Statistics show that 42% in Asia, 39% in Africa, and 27% in Latin America live in what the ILO terms absolute poverty. Most of these people (85%) still live in rural areas, although the number of landless people trekking to urban areas is increasing.

Poverty and malnourishment go hand in hand. While few drop dead from starvation, chronic hunger exacts a terrible toll. In some areas half the children can expect to die of hunger-related illnesses.[3] The chronically hungry have less resistance to disease and are more susceptible to parasites. The children of the poor are 15 times more likely to die before their first birthday. Protein deficiency, marasmus, goiter, pellagra, beriberi, vitamin-A deficiency, blindness, and permanent mental damage are all problems associated with chronic hunger.

The statistics go on to fill volumes, but seldom do they reveal the human misery and pain which they represent. Promising lives cut short, families with lost or deformed children, and the hopelessness of seeing no way out combine to form a landscape of dehumanization comparable to the holocaust and the cross. In the midst of this landscape many Americans drive along, feet on their accelerators, worried about the price of gasoline or hamburger. It is not that Americans are more insensitive than other people. There may be some of this, but it is more a matter of priorities, of where attention is directed. Returning to the analogy of the car on the superhighway, it is as if the attention of Americans is being consumed by the sheer number of activities needed to keep getting and going. Keeping the car on the road, maneuvering it out of the way of other vehicles, and aiming it in the right direction demand attention. Distractions lead to accidents, and world poverty and malnutrition are often distractions to Americans.

Poverty, the Main Cause of Hunger

To the popular imagination the world food problem is a matter of too many people, too little land, and unpredictable climate. That these factors are at work in the present situation is undeniable. Having said this, it is important to recognize that these three factors are not the primary causes of malnutrition. The fact is, even in years of the most severe climatic changes, more than sufficient food is and has been available to feed all the world's people. Frances Moore Lappé and Joseph Collins, using readily available statistics, calculate the world's production of food even during the worst years of the 1970s at more than 3000 calories per person, a figure above the average American intake.[4] Moreover, the rate of growth of food production has substantially exceeded population growth in each of the last three decades, even in many of the poorest countries.[5] What these simple statistics reveal is a basic fact about malnutrition: there is plenty of food to go around. Why then is there such physical suffering? The key to answering this question lies in the dynamics of population growth and food production.

The present 1.7% per year increase in world population, encouragingly down from a 2% figure just a few years ago, is a consequence of rapidly decreased death rates and not so rapidly decreasing birth rates. The decreased death rates are a blessing brought by modern medicine, public health, and improved sanitation. That birth rates have not kept pace in a downward direction is not surprising given the slowness of social change in traditional societies. Common sense would seem to suggest, however, that high birth rates and low death rates are a prescription for disaster which everyone can see.

While common sense is correct in the long range, it is misapplied in the short. It overlooks the reasons why people continue to have more than two or three children. It is not so much a matter of contraception, ignorance, or lack of willpower, although these play a small role. Simply put, poor men and women have more than two or three children because they are landless and without economic security. Children do not eliminate poverty, but they do spread the burden of work, earn income even at an early age, and provide the only security available in old age, if, that is, their parents are prudent enough to have many of them so a few survive. The often cited figure is six children to ensure a single surviving male offspring. More-over, the benefits of children are gained at the expense of only another mouth to feed, not an insurmountable burden normally. The children of the poor do not go to pediatricians. Nor do they need strollers, elaborate wardrobes, and college educations. They are thus a benefit with few costs. Economic necessity dictates high birth rates.

In other words, poverty and the quest of economic security are the root causes of high birth rates, not the reverse, as in the popular imagination. This being the case, the antidote for high population growth rates is the attainment of economic security by poor people. This solution receives additional support from the experiences of countries which have gone through the industrialization process. Almost without exception the attainment of economic security has brought in its train significantly lowered birth rates even without elaborate contraception and educational programs.[6]

Having made this observation, it is advisable to take a few steps back from it. The attainment of economic security does not necessarily mean economic development along the road taken by industrialized countries. Not only does this form of development have ecologically destructive side effects, but it is also the carrier of wrenching social and cultural changes, not all of which are desirable. It can also lead, in the absence of social reform, to greater impoverishment of the poor.

Turning to the food production side of the ledger, the primacy of economic causes is again revealed. Taken alone, the statistics on food production in many Third World countries would suggest that a dramatic reduction in malnutrition has occurred. Big production gains have resulted from the so-called green revolution, an integrated approach to increasing the yields of food crops which makes use of new seed varieties, mechanization, irrigation, fertilizer, and pesticides. All is not well with the green revolution, however. In many poor countries the green revolution has actually resulted in greater poverty and malnutrition. Hunger in the midst of ample food production: this is a paradox that needs explanation.

One view of this paradox sees it as a failure by the poor to exploit new production possibilities. In this view low production rates in poor countries are a consequence of plots which are

too small, population densities which are too high, and a failure
to supply the right inputs.[7]

While there is truth in this view, a more in-depth investiga-
tion reveals its superficiality. Small plots in many poor countries have higher yields per acre than large plots.[8] In fact, the
number a given piece of land will feed depends not so much on
the size of plots as the level of investment in human beings to
increase production; on whether the land is used to feed people
or livestock; on whether the land grows luxury crops for export
or food for local consumption; and on the ownership or control
of the land.[9]

As for population densities, there seems to be little relationship between density and output. From most reports China's
900 million are adequately nourished. Japan and Taiwan, with
twice as many agricultural workers per acre as the Philippines
and India, have much higher productivity per acre.[10] India with
172 inhabitants per square kilometer outproduces Bolivia with a
population density of five per square kilometer.[11]

Finally, the claim that farmers have failed to supply the right
inputs misses the real dynamics. True, the green revolution and
mechanization have produced dramatic gains in production. To
realize these gains, however, ample water, fertilizer, and pesticides are required. These cost money which is precisely what the
poor do not have. Ample water in many regions depends on expensive irrigation systems. Fertilizer derived from petroleum is
costly. Pesticides come mostly from the developed countries and
are expensive to import. The seeds themselves require a considerable investment. Quite simply, the rich or the government
supported, often the same people, are the only ones able to afford
these inputs. Lappé and Collins sum up the effect of the green
revolution as follows:

> We have now arrived at the endpoint of the tragic decline of
> the rural majority. In country after country, where agricultural
> resources are allowed to be sources of private wealth, the drive
> to increase food production has made even worse the lives of
> the poor majority, despite per capita increases. We have seen
> how:
>
> —Land values go up, forcing tenants and small farmers off
> the land.
>
> —Rents increase.

—Payments in money become the rule, yet money buys less food.

—The control of the farmland becomes concentrated in fewer hands, many of whom are speculative entrepreneurs, not farmers.

—Even communal areas are appropriated by . . . individuals . . . for their private gain at the expense of the welfare of the community.

—Corporate control, often foreign, extends further into production.

—Peasants are trapped into debt bondage.

—Poverty and inequality deepen.

—Production totals, not the participation of the rural population in the production process . . . become the measure of success. . . .

—Quantity and market value, not nutritive value, become the goal of agricultural planning.[12]

One conclusion is inescapable. Concentration on production alone is not the answer to the problem of poverty and malnutrition. The green revolution is important and should be adapted to local needs, but before it can help the estimated 700 million in absolute poverty other things must happen. According to Susan George:

So long as thoroughgoing land reform and distribution of resources to the poorest . . . does not take place, Third World countries can go on increasing their production until hell freezes, and hunger will remain, for the production will go to those who have plenty. . . .[13]

The Colonial Heritage

The green revolution is an amalgamation of new agricultural technologies. It is not in itself to blame for hunger and poverty. Yet it is an excellent example of the profound social consequences of modern technology to be explored in the next chapter. Designed and implemented according to narrow technical and economic specifications, little account has been given in most countries to wider social consequences. The flaw is not so much in the technologies themselves as in the way certain nations, often with the encouragement of Americans, organize their productive resources. The probe into the paradox of hunger in the midst of ample food production must go still deeper.

The extremes of wealth and poverty in most developing countries, concentration of land ownership, and a pattern of dependence on cash crops for export are a reality and were so long before the green revolution. In many countries a pattern of agriculture developed in colonial periods and persists to this day. The pattern had two main features: concentration on a single, or at most a few, crops which were needed in the colonizing country, and production of these crops on large estates. This pattern was often established at the expense of a diversifed agricultural system that had earlier more than supported the local population.

This colonial pattern left an indelible mark. It left transportation systems designed to move export goods. It also left a system of cash cropping in which the best land and resources are given to the production of commodities for export to developed countries. Cocoa in Ghana, peanuts in Gambia, rubber in Liberia, palm oil in Tanzania, bananas and more recently specialty vegetables and beef in Latin America—the list goes on and on. This system bears heavy blame for the paradox of hunger in the midst of ample food production and for the stagnation of the peasant food-producing sector. Recently it has not served the cash crop producers all that well either, as the terms of trade have worsened for commodities over against manufactured goods. Many developing countries are finding themselves required to devote ever-increasing resources to cash crops just to maintain export income needed to pay off massive debts.

The colonial system also concentrated ownership of the land. A small wealthy class has benefited enormously, forming a community of interest with importers in developed countries at the expense of the landless poor. This class and its allies in the emerging urban middle class have been the real beneficiaries of cash cropping, economic expansion, and the green revolution.[14] Furthermore, this class is frequently supported, and its power enhanced, by the military aid of the United States and its allies, by multinationals, and more recently by the green revolution and mechanization. It is a system well designed for the benefit of the few. It helps the poor directly very little and indirectly hurts them a great deal, if nothing else by diverting resources.

Agrarian Reform

It would be simplistic to claim that poverty, inappropriate technologies, and the colonial heritage are the sole causes of hunger, high birth rates, and economic insecurity. Besides these, inadequate land and water resources, the absence of non-agricultural employment, mistaken priorities, the force of local custom, and the sheer pressure of too many people continually recur as causes in surveys of countries with large numbers of poor people. In addition, there are problems unique to each situation. But no matter how many factors are involved, poverty and malnutrition will not be reduced short of major social changes in both developed and developing countries. These changes must be paid for in the ancient coin of social justice; that is, in a change of priorities which puts the elimination of hunger and poverty first and removes the pattern of colonial domination.

Agrarian reform is a term used to describe a general package which has served the aims of justice in several countries, notably China, Taiwan, Sri Lanka, and at times in its history, Mexico. It has three main components: 1) land reform, 2) technical modernization, and 3) credit and marketing support services.[15] The main thrust of land reform is to redistribute land for the benefit of small farmers and landless agricultural workers. Governments or local cooperatives acquire land either by confiscation or payment to the owners and redistribute it by grants to individuals or collectives. Land reform accompanied by participative decision making results in lower birth rates and increased productivity. These gains are due to the new relation to the land and economic security which reform brings, not to changes in the size of landholdings. Production and distribution become matters of self-interest to the poor.

Land reform alone is not sufficient. Unless backup services are in place, the tendency is to slip back into old patterns. Poor farmers increase their debt, ownership is defaulted, and the old pattern of concentration returns. Support services are of two kinds, technical and financial. Included in the former are technical modernization, research on local conditions, education and health services, improved nutrition and family planning, and area development projects.[16] Technical modernization does not necessarily mean complex, energy-intensive new equipment. For example, a rototiller and a good oxplow are as good as a tractor;

mixed cropping and organic fertilizers are as good as chemical fertilizers. The requirement is for technologies suited to local needs and capacities. These seldom need to be large in scale or complex in nature.

Credit and marketing services also are essential.[17] Without credit, small farmers have no way of using newly acquired land. Credit must also be integrated with extension services and marketing promotion. Agricultural cooperatives are useful organizations for these purposes. Finally, adequate storage facilities and price stabilization are necessary for security and planning.

The obstacles to agrarian reform are internal and external. Land reform is naturally opposed by large landowners even when they are adequately compensated. Unfortunately, the wherewithal for compensation is not readily available in poor countries. But confiscation runs up against constitutional questions and the struggle to maintain the rule of law. Implementation of land reform often suffers from a lack of trained administrators. Support services require a heavy investment in human beings and physical capital, for which trained personnel again are not available. In addition, there are competing priorities. Agrarian reform vies with the industrial sector for investment capital. Externally, worsening terms of trade, inadequate and inappropriate aid, and the interference of foreign governments and corporations with different priorities frustrate reform.

These obstacles do not lead to a sense of hopelessness. Gains in food production have been made in all but the poorest countries. Birth rates are dropping slowly. Productivity is up. Most countries have made at least minimal efforts at land reform. Experts are becoming more sophisticated about the complexity of the problem and the need to tailor solutions to local needs. Perhaps the biggest hope lies in the people. If through agrarian reform the conditions can be established which make broadly based participation and self-reliance possible, declining birth rates and increased production of food by the poor should follow. To establish these conditions, one prerequisite is a sense of urgency about social justice.

The North American Response

North American Christians have a role to play. The role they are now playing is ambiguous. On the one hand, several church

organizations have been working innovatively on these problems. Bread for the World, Church World Service through its
crop hunger appeals, Catholic Relief Services, and Lutheran
World Relief are just a few of many Christian organizations
working on a small scale. While their resources are too limited
for addressing the problems on a mass scale, they are making a
difference in a few local areas and providing models and a training ground for an expanded effort.

On the other hand, Christians, like most other North Americans, are contributing to the problems. Their contributions are
often indirect and little understood. Some contribute by pursuing the interests of their business in the opinion that their
efforts are helping the poor. The vast majority contribute by
small everyday acts whose impacts on the poor are overlooked.
A few are quite consciously exploiting the poor for their own
self-interest.

All North Americans contribute unwittingly through their
consumption habits. On the average North Americans consume
2000 pounds of grain per person per year. By comparison, in
the developing countries the figure is approximately 400 pounds.
One reason why some do not have food in a world with ample
production is because others are consuming beef and other foodstuffs at prodigious rates.

North Americans contribute in still other ways. They naturally
pursue their self-interest and purchase food at the lowest price.
Several crops can only be grown in tropical countries. Many
crops are grown more cheaply in poor countries. North Americans demand these products. Their demand stimulates production of certain commodities in developing countries which then
become cash crops for export. Agents, often representatives of
large corporations, encourage production in cash crops along
highly mechanized lines. Income flows to corporations and
wealthy landholders. The poor retreat to urban slums or live
on the margins of the land.

This is an oversimplified schema, of course, and the primary
blame may rest on international economic organizations working in alliance with wealthy landholders. Yet the fact remains,
North American Christians are benefiting from and contributing
to the problem through their consumption.

Not all observers agree. In support of present arrangements
and in opposition to the charge that North Americans overcon-

sume, University of Chicago economist D. Gale Johnson argues that increased North American demand has actually stimulated overall food production through higher prices and thus helped the poor.[18] To reduce this demand, warns Johnson, would be to reduce overall production and to increase poverty and hunger.

It is also clear that cutting consumption will not put the resulting surplus in the stomachs of the poor. Given present arrangements, the surplus will either be eaten by others with less scruples or go to waste and never reach the poor for lack of purchasing power. Lower consumption would also reduce farm prices both here and abroad, thus hurting farmers and reducing incentives in all countries.

Unless accompanied by agrarian reform or food aid tailored to the complexities of local situations, decreasing consumption by North Americans is a gesture which does not immediately help the poor and malnourished. That it may have other positive impacts such as calling awareness to the problems of world hunger, preparing public opinion, and improved nutrition cannot be denied. But again, this puts precious little food in hungry stomachs. Only reduced consumption coupled with social change will work.

Turning to the role of American agribusiness and multinational corporations, critics charge these organizations with abuses ranging from supporting wealthy landholders against the landless poor, to perpetuating the colonial heritage, to importing technologies whose side effects are devastating on the poor, to outright exploitation. More moderately a United Nations study had this to say:

> There has been a tendency for transnational businesses to encourage a particular model of development. This, while it modernizes the agriculture of specific export-oriented crops, sometimes causes a detrimental change of agrarian structure. By concentrating capital, credit and technical assistance on large units of the best land, transnational corporations often reap marked increases in agricultural output and productivity; the pattern of growth which they foster, however, is often very uneven, regionally and in respect of products, as well as technology used, and leads in some cases to unhealthy economic and social fixations. In some cases their activities have been found to retard the integration of rural/urban sectors of the national economy.[19]

In defense of agribusinesses and other multinationals, they seldom create the conditions in which they operate. They do not normally select the leaders of developing countries, although there have been occasions when their influence has been more than casual. Finally, it would be unusual for these organizations to behave differently. They conceive their task to be the pursuit of profits and the provision of markets for already developed countries. According to their perspective, buying cheap and selling dear, in keeping with accepted economic logic, helps everyone. That it negatively impacts the poor in developing countries is either passed off as lamentable or denied by pointing to all the jobs which their economic activity creates and the lower prices they make possible.

That North Americans gain advantage at the expense of the poor is further revealed in the worsening terms of trade experienced by most developing countries. North Americans are generally unaware of this, since rising prices at the food market and the worsening balance of trade with other developed countries and OPEC nations dominate press accounts. That very few poor countries participate in the OPEC windfall except negatively through higher energy costs goes unrealized. The statistics tell the story. During the period of 1953-1976 the terms of trade of the developing countries over a broad range of exports declined 1.7% per year according to World Bank estimates.[20] This is caused largely by the protection developed countries give to the production of finished goods and the dependence of less developed countries on raw materials and cash crops sold in competitive markets. These worsening terms of trade have meant increased dependency on cash crops. Poor nations must export more and more just to maintain balance and to pay off past debts. It has also meant the frustration of development plans due to uncertainty about income.

The last way in which North Americans contribute to the problem is through their aid programs. Development assistance, as measured by the ability to give, has been miserly and often inappropriate due to design difficulties and trouble grasping the nature of the problems. The right kind of aid in sufficient quantity is essential to relieving poverty and malnutrition. The record is not good. Discounting direct military aid, which varies from year to year between $2 and $6 billion and does nothing to help the poor, the contribution of the United States to de-

velopment assistance dropped in real terms from $4 billion in
1963 to $1.84 billion in 1973 and remains at approximately that
level today. If total aid is considered, including Food for Peace,
the Peace Corps, and paid-in subscriptions to international financial institutions, the figure is much higher: $4.1 billion in 1973
and $9.7 billion in 1980, the latter figure not adjusted for infla-
tion.[21] In per capita terms this level of aid puts the United
States well down on the list of nations giving aid.[22] In addition,
this aid has been aimed for the most part at development projects
which recreate American methods. Little of it has trickled down
to the poor; the main beneficiaries have been the wealthy landowners, the small urban upper class, and North American
corporations.

The United States also gives aid in the form of food. Under
Title I of Public Law 480, low interest loans or credits are granted to friendly countries who then purchase United States commodities and sell them on local markets. These loans have
helped several countries make up shortfalls and relieve infla-
tionary pressures, but the selling of food on local markets means
the poor who are without purchasing power are excluded.

Under Title II of Public Law 480, food may be given away
for emergency famine relief. This aid has saved many lives but
does not get at the real cause of poverty and malnutrition. In
fact, food loans and giveaways, if extended over long periods of
time, create dependency and reduce prices and incentives. With
the exception of famine situations, giving food away is one of
the worst policies. Giveaways should halt at first opportunity in
order to promote self-reliant food production.

In assessing United States food aid, consideration must be
given to its originally stated purpose: "to develop and expand
export markets for United States agricultural commodities." In
other words, the purpose of food aid has until recently been to
unload surpluses and to obtain dependable food markets. Public
Law 480 makes no appeal to justice and little to humanitarian-
ism. This is also true of the political uses to which food surpluses
have been put; for example, the large quantity of aid sent in the
1970s to a few politically sensitive friends such as Egypt and
South Vietnam. Recent changes in Public Law 480 have moved
this balance in a humanitarian direction, but it is too early to
tell if actual practice will shift.

International lending institutions such as the World Bank

have picked up some of the slack left by declining United States development assistance. The United States contributes to, and in many cases exerts heavy influence on, these institutions whose records with regard to the poor have been improving. The World Bank has recently set itself the task of significantly increasing the forms of aid which get at the root causes of poverty and malnutrition. This follows a long period in which the policy was to funnel aid through local power groups to projects with little or no impact on the poor.

Changing Responses

The attitude that immediate solutions to hunger and poverty are available and that Americans are the best problem solvers is a dangerous attitude. The problems run deep, and doing things "for" poor people instead of "with" them will be of little help. It is impossible here to draw up a checklist of acceptable and unacceptable practices to be applied to some generalized country. Local variations and needs render abstract programs irrelevant. It is not possible to detail the political steps by which practices injurious to the world's poor and malnourished could be stopped. Certainly action by the less developed countries themselves to prevent negative external intrusions is a *sine qua non.* But this begs the question because power is held in so many cases by those who benefit from accustomed patterns of aid and the investment patterns of multinationals. Short of a basic reorientation of power and a new ethic, both in the United States and in developing countries, prospects for stopping these intrusions are not good. Yet there are several steps North Americans can take to reduce their contribution to the problems and to increase the chances for economic security and better nutrition.

The first step is to understand the problems and to discard the attitude of doing things "for" the poor. The second step is to stop practices which contribute to the misery of the poor; for example, the introduction and dissemination of complex, large-scale technologies when technologies scaled to end uses and to the needs of the poor are more appropriate; the support of governments which make "food first" a low priority; and exploitive practices of multinationals.

Step three is more active and positive. It involves giving of food and increased economic assistance. For all that has been said against doing things "for" the poor, increased aid is still essential. Present levels of aid are miserly. But increased aid is not enough. It must be carefully coupled with agrarian reform and targeted to the needs of the rural poor, otherwise it will be siphoned off by those in power. Aid programs must promote self-reliance and be carefully assessed for their impact on farm prices and incentives. Food aid should be given only in emergencies and in periods of serious shortfalls to avoid dependency and lower farm prices.

One form of aid that makes good sense is investment in local agricultural development projects that are tied to agrarian reform. Since agrarian reform requires investment in capital and financial support services, economic assistance could be used in off seasons to employ farm workers in building such things as irrigation systems and fertilizer plants. It could also be used to provide low interest loans and credit to individual farmers or farm cooperatives.

Former Central Intelligence Agency Director William Colby has proposed an innovative program modeled on the Food Stamp program in the United States but designed for the less developed countries in Latin America.[23] Stamps given directly to the poor would be used on the open market to purchase food. This would put purchasing power where it is needed and stimulate local farm production. If local inflation threatens because of increased demand, surplus American foodstuffs could be imported and sold for food stamps in order to stabilize prices. This feature would be attractive to American farmers and at the same time maintain local prices at fairly high levels. Colby overlooks the problem of dependency in his plan by advocating direct grants, but his program could be adapted to increase self-reliance by using the stamps as payment for work projects.

Another form of aid is basic research which will support agrarian reform and promote the production of food for the hungry instead of cash crops for the rich. Research designed to improve seed varieties and their adaptation to local farming techniques, to promote the introduction of technologies scaled to local needs and capabilities, and to educate the concepts of total crop utilization are badly needed. The cost of such research is not great and the research itself could be conducted in regional centers located within poor countries. This would help to avoid the kind of training often received in the United States which emphasizes mechanization, large-scale technologies, and sophisticated technical knowledge.

Although it involves no direct giving, another form of aid is trade liberalization and the granting of temporary advantages to less developed countries. This is an issue in and of itself and revolves around the call for a New International Economic Order (NIEO).[24] Basically the NIEO involves the following advantages for less developed countries:

1. Improved terms of trade for commodities and raw materials.
2. Increased access to and availability of affordable credit.
3. Improved access to markets in developed countries, including lower tariffs on manufactured goods.
4. The promotion of industrialization.
5. The transfer of technology from developed to less developed countries.
6. The regulation of multinationals.
7. The promotion of cooperation among less developed countries.

There may be quarrels with specifics in this proposal and questions about whether it takes into sufficient account the problems associated with modern technology, the maldistribution of wealth and power within developing countries, or a policy of food first, but it at least points to some of the abuses which have frustrated development plans.

Listing the different forms of possible aid is one thing, seeing them realized in effective programs is quite another. Technical and economic roadblocks are minor when compared to the political opposition which will materialize. Other things being equal, any significant aid package would entail higher taxes or prices or both in the nation giving aid. Given the present climate of tax revolt, suspicion of governmental initiatives, and low rates of growth in the United States, a significant aid package is not immediately likely. Nor is it made more so by the powerful special interests with which it must contend. Multinationals can be counted on to fight attempts to break up profitable arrangements. Consumer groups will oppose higher grocery prices. Farmers will reject any program that raises their costs or lowers their prices. Labor groups are constantly wary of trade liberalization which throws domestic workers out of jobs. From the perspectives of the individuals involved, resistance is understandable. No one wants to bear the brunt of sacrifice for the poor. Each

thinks it is a matter of justice that his or her interests not be
sacrificed. But looking at it from the side of the poor, the refusal
to give appears as national selfishness.

To make a dent in the armor of group interests many Christians have elected simplified ways of living. Aside from improved
health from eating less of some foods, the chief values of changing
consumption habits are spiritual and symbolic. Spiritually, simplified ways of living put the Christian closer both to the poor
and to the New Testament ideal of voluntary poverty and freedom from possessions. Symbolically, these changes call attention
to the plight of the poor and to the preoccupation of Americans
with consumption. They keep alive a sense of sharing and proportion and leave open the possibility of further social transformation.

In theory, changed ways of living also free up resources for
alternatives such as development assistance. Reduced consumption of material goods produces excess productive capacity which
can be used to manufacture goods for the poor. The eating of
less beef frees up grain for hungry people, or so the argument
goes. In fact, as we have seen, reduced consumption does nothing
of the kind in the absence of specific initiatives to transfer productive capacity and to achieve greater levels of justice. Short of
such initiatives, reduced consumption produces unemployment
at home and abroad and reduces prices, enabling heavy consumers to consume even more. Indeed, a change in life-style as
a strategy by itself is congenial to the status quo. It does nothing
to bring about the structural changes needed in a more just
world. Arthur Simon, executive director of Bread for the World,
sums it up by saying, "a life-style adjustment may be useful, but
detached from attempts to influence government policy, it tends
to be an ineffective gesture. Our sense of stewardship must become sufficiently large for both." [25]

Poverty and malnutrition are complex problems admitting no
easy solutions. Even the word *solution* is misplaced, for the
transformation, productivity increases, and lower birth rates
needed for solution are staggering. Amelioration or reduction of
the problems is a realistic goal, however. It requires the combined efforts of rich and poor. In less developed countries this
means agrarian reform and commitment to the self-reliant development of the poor. In the developed countries it means the
cessation of exploitive practices, new forms and greater quantity

of aid, and changed patterns of living. In all countries it means
a commitment to social justice. At present the political will for
such mammoth transformation is weak.

Fortunately social problems are more than a mere calculation
of economic and political feasibility. There are other dimensions. Few relish the role of exploiter. The American people can
be generous once problems are made clear. Individuals are band-
ing together in action groups to influence policy. In other words,
resources are available, and among the most significant are the
resources of the Christian tradition and the work of the Holy
Spirit. The Spirit is at work wherever love and justice are living
realities. The Christian tradition is rich in precisely those ways
of thinking and being which are now called for: liberation, justice, concern for the poor, sharing, and participation in community.

For the poor and the hungry the Christian message is one of
hope. God does not neglect human suffering. God resists arro-
gance, responds to the humble, and calls humans in their freedom to protect the weak, to limit the strong, and to reconcile
the two in justice. For North American Christians as a whole
this is a message of judgment, for it is they who are among the
strong and the arrogant. The judgment of God is a powerful
brake on the superhighway assumptions of Americans. That
judgment is now being heard through the voices of the poor, and
Christians here and there are putting on their brakes and beginning to listen to these voices.

Justice is the key. The just society in light of the Bible is:

> A society in which the cry of human hope and suffering are
> heard. We are responsible more to realize justice than to use
> it for our own advantage. Justice is never a static self-defense,
> but always a dynamic creation. Justice is never definitively
> established, but always a search in the fear and the hope of
> the judgment of God, which brings liberation and redemption,
> forgiveness and health.[26]

CHAPTER 3

Technology and Participation

Mike Mulligan and His Steam Shovel is a classic 1939 children's story.[1] Mike is the proud owner and operator of a bright red steam shovel named Mary Anne. According to Mike, Mary Anne can dig as much in a day as a hundred men can in a week. By modern standards of efficiency not much to look at, Mary Anne at least has her name personally painted on her boom in bold white letters. Her happy face tells children she is something more than a machine, an "almost" person, at very least someone who will listen in and play. Mary Anne is also a powerful shovel. With Mike and a few others she digs canals, cuts railroads through mountain passes, smooths hills for superhighways, and turns pastures into airport runways, all in the name of progress.

Surprisingly, the illustrations which accompany the story do not reveal much of Mary Anne's face when she is at work. More troublesome, the canals which Mike and Mary Anne dig have no bridges to link former neighbors. Presumably the people living on what are now the two sides of the canal were so impressed that separation from one another was no cause for concern. As for the train billowing black smoke and ash in pristine mountain passes, only the hikers and the deer seem to care, and they appear to be hailing the speeding locomotive as a savior, not as an intruder.

The illustration of Mike and Mary Anne leveling the hills for a new superhighway is perhaps the most revealing of all. It speaks volumes about how Americans have prized a narrow form of technical and economic progress and neglected what lies beside the road or stands in the background. In this illustration Mike and Mary Anne are drawing the reader's attention by digging furiously in the foreground. What they are digging into are the beautiful green front lawns of the houses which stand unnoticed in the background. In the next illustration the highway is completed and a dozen or so vehicles are speeding along in the foreground. Again in the background unnoticed are the houses now shorn of their lawns. The text mentions nothing of the people who live in these houses and whether they had a say in the road construction or were consulted about the noise and air pollution. Presumably, to the mind of 1939, these things were inconsequential.

The next pages bring the inevitable adversity. Enter with the latest technology three new shovels powered by gasoline, diesel fuel, and electricity. The text matter-of-factly notes that the new shovels "took all the jobs away from the steam shovels," a note whose simplicity masks a very important assumption. That assumption is the inevitability of social change brought by new technology. No one decides whether Mary Anne and her class of technology are to be superseded. They just are, and, as if directed by an "invisible hand," the whole process is supposed to work out for the best.

The faces on the new shovels are not so invisible. In contrast to Mary Anne's very human smiling, crying, and sweating, the new shovels have a haughty, impersonal, and cool look. Their eyes are closed and their noses stuck up. Clearly the reader is being told that new technology, however efficient, does not relate with the warmth of Mary Anne to Mike. The close personalism of Mike and Mary Anne is replaced by cool efficiency. Symbolically, only one man is visible in the illustration of the new shovels, and he is not the center of attention.

The next illustration shows Mike and Mary Anne peeping over the precipice down into the junk heap of obsolete and abandoned steam shovels. Mary Anne's mouth droops as she contemplates her fate, and Mike is beside himself with anguish. Presumably the reader sympathizes with Mike and Mary Anne, but progress is progress and the old, be they people or machines,

must give way to the new and retire to carefully segregated junkyards.

Mike and Mary Anne are, of course, spared this fate. Mike
reads an advertisement placed by the Selectmen of Popperville,
a small town far away from the canals, railroads, highways, and
new shovels. The citizens of Popperville have decided to build
a new town hall and need a shovel for excavation work. But
Popperville is not so far away as to be off the highway of progress. Incredibly, the citizens of this typically pastoral New England town have chosen the commons, the one grassy place left
in the center of town, for the location of their new town hall.
Instead of grassy places at the center of their life together, they
have chosen a building and apparently have done so without
a dissenting vote.

Mike and Mary Anne are chosen. A wager is made that Mike
and Mary Anne cannot complete the excavation work in one day.
They begin with the rising of the sun and, against all odds,
finish the task as the sun sets. Unfortunately they have mis-
calculated. They have left no way out of the pit they have dug.
All ends happily in spite of this unfortunate twist. Mary Anne
becomes the heating plant for the new town hall and Mike the
custodian. It is a fitting retirement, and both live happily ever
after.

1939 was a different age. Today there would be court battles
over the location of the town hall. Obsolete people are not re-
tiring quietly to junkyards. Homeowners are not standing idly
by as the state runs a highway through their front yards. Environmentalists decry the rape of wilderness areas. Canal build-
ers are forced to provide connecting links. Today social goals
are in dispute. Technological innovation is no longer accepted
as automatically progressive. Yet the forces producing and pushing new technologies are still everywhere in place. Witness the
current fascination with computers.

The problem is technology in the broad sense of the word.
Narrowly conceived, technology is the application of scientific
knowledge to the practical problems of producing goods and
services. In a broader sense, specific technologies are part of a
human process which also includes economic structures, political
arrangements, ideas, and values. It is the dehumanizing power
and the seeming inevitability of the larger process which is causing so much discontent.

Technology and the Problem of Participation

The value of participation has been the focal point for this discontent in World Council discussions. At the most obvious level participation means sharing in community decisions, the assumption being that high levels of personal interaction improve individual well-being and the functioning of communities. This is the obvious intent of a 1977 World Council gathering in Switzerland which in its report first stated its theological presuppositions.

> If we seek a biblical basis for participation, we may find it in the concepts of "covenant" and "communion." According to the Bible, God reigns not by imposed domination but by confirmed covenant with his people and he draws his people into communion with each other and himself. To participate is therefore to move further in an unfinished enterprise that is the common history of God with human freedom and of humanity with the divine purpose. Participation is the expression of membership in a common body. . . .
>
> In this light a "participatory" society may be interpreted as a society in which the community is neither imposed nor forgotten, in which decisions are shared and also in which the processes of sharing are not the means to postpone decisions.[2]

Mike and Mary Anne, for all their personality, ignore participation in community. Nameless and distant persons, presumably using economic criteria, decide the construction projects which Mike and Mary Anne faithfully carry out. "They" ignore the bridges needed to link the people separated by canals. "They" cut through mountains, route highways through front yards, and consign steam shovels to junk heaps, all without consultation.

To the market economist this is as it should be. The "they" is each of us making "free" economic choices in the market place. This is the most efficient and painless way to decide. Participation is casting dollar votes. This is where freedom is to be exercised.

This is not the place to go into the merits of market capitalism. Suffice it to say that the World Council discussions have sought a deeper sense of participation than the mere exercise of choice

among products. In these discussions the theological basis has
been the notions of freedom and responsibility. Freedom at its
most basic level is the freedom of faith. It is the liberation which
comes from receiving and responding to the love of God. This
freedom is the freedom from bondage to sin and the freedom for
others in the resurrection of Jesus Christ. This form of freedom
is possible whether or not political and economic freedoms are
present. Nevertheless, the absence of political and economic freedoms hampers the ability of a person to respond (responsibility)
to God's love. It is difficult to respond with love when one's
existence is determined by others or by impersonal market forces.

God's love therefore has to do not only with the redemption of
individuals, but also with political and economic liberation. God
works to create the conditions for the free exercise of personal
responsibility. God, according to theologian Shubert Ogden,
"intends the fullest possible self-realization of each of his creatures and infallibly acts to do all that can be done to that end—
save only what his creatures themselves have to do, both for themselves and for one another."[3]

Political and economic liberty, that is, the opportunity to respond within a community setting to God and to other persons,
is thus a presupposition of effective participation. The 1948
Amsterdam Assembly of the World Council, in its declaration on
the responsible society, put it this way:

> Man is created and called to be a free being, responsible to
> God and his neighbor. Any tendencies in State and society
> depriving man of the possibility of acting responsibly are a
> denial of God's intention for man and his work of salvation.
> A responsible society is one where freedom is the freedom of
> men who acknowledge responsibility to justice and public
> order, and where those who hold political authority or eco-
> nomic power are responsible for its exercise to God and the
> people whose welfare is affected by it.
>
> Man must never be made a mere means for political or eco-
> nomic ends. Man is not made for the State but the State for
> man. Man is not made for production, but production for
> man. For a society to be responsible under modern conditions
> it is required that the people have freedom to control, to
> criticize and to change their governments, that power be made
> responsible by law and tradition, and be distributed as widely
> as possible through the whole community. It is required that

economic justice and provision of equality of opportunity be established for all the members of society.[4]

The problem in developed countries stems from the dominance of economic and technological factors in community decisions; for example, the decision to replace steam shovels with newer, high-performance shovels. This domination is without apparent direction or goal. It is the consequence of a unique historical convergence which transformed Western society from one dominated by tradition to another dominated by the pursuit of means, namely wealth and efficiency. No one really "chose" this transformation. Thousands of uncoordinated, individual decisions combined to produce it. Few, if any, of the decision makers were aware of the larger whole which they were creating. Once established, this new society imposed and continues to impose certain social structures, means of interaction, and values. It is the directionless imposition of these structures, interactions, and values without meaningful participation that is the problem.

For some observers, like French sociologist Jacques Ellul, there has been a grand reversal. Technological means have become the motor of social change. For others, like economist John Kenneth Galbraith, a small coterie of technically trained people manipulate technologies with their own welfare in mind. For still others, exemplified by political scientist Langdon Winner, "drift" is the word which best characterizes the situation. Technological society is without controls, drifting about at the mercy of uncoordinated forces.

In the less developed countries modern technology threatens to tear apart the frail body of participation already worked over by colonialism, maldistribution, and dependency. The magnitude of the problem is revealed in a list of criteria for inappropriate technology put together by a multi-world working group at the World Council Conference at M.I.T.

Technology is inappropriate according to the Report of the Conference if:

    i) it leads to absorption or destruction of national industries;

    ii) it suppresses the domestic market for indigenous products;

    iii) it redeploys resources and facilities from use by the majority to enhance the prestige and luxury of a few;

    iv) it introduces unnecessary hazards and risks through obsolete or harmful designs and products;

v) it encourages the creation of unnecessary desires and ur-
   banization;

vi) it cannot be assimilated or controlled by national techni-
    cians but remains an intimidating and alienating force
    deepening dependence;

vii) it stifles the national independent research and develop-
     ment which alone can ensure long-term technological self-
     reliance;

viii) it exploits natural resources without regard to the long-
      term needs of the country and its environment;

ix) it intensifies existing class divisions in the society and
    entrenches the status quo;

x) it displaces workers and offers no desirable employment
   alternative, i.e., if it creates "technological unemployment." [5]

Large-scale, complex, energy and capital intensive technologies
are beyond the ability of people untrained in modern practices to
understand and use. They practically guarantee reduced levels
of sharing in vital community decisions.

To be sure, modernization does not eliminate participation.
In fact, it creates new forms of participation, but often these
forms are not as adequate as the ones they replace. Often they
are more impersonal. Mass spectator sports, television, and the
automobile are examples. With spectator sports, anonymous participation is no substitute for the personalized caring of small
communities. Television and automobiles interpose material objects between persons who, in a traditional society, would never
have interacted, or had they, would have done so in a direct man-
ner. The greater mobility provided by modern forms of transportation opens a vast number of new contacts to those who can
afford them. But these contacts are frequently superficial, and
mobility itself reduces community cohesiveness.

Policymakers are caught on the horns of a dilemma. On the one
hand the requirements of maintaining the technological process
demand the very actions which decrease participation: detailed
planning by technically competent managers; huge amounts of
capital; precise and detailed definition of complex tasks; and
specialized and well-trained experts. These demands, or so-called
imperatives of technology, usually dictate big, impersonal, and
powerful organizations with an hierarchical chain of management. The managers and technical experts themselves participate

in decisions, but the participation of persons outside organizational boundaries only confuses and prolongs decision making. The power of these large organizations is extensive and creates an imbalance in power arrangements, further worsening the situation.

On the other hand, policymakers are forced to hear the voices of those who do not participate in technical decisions. The steam shovels are fighting back, so to speak. Homeowners and environmentalists resist new highways. Airports are difficult to locate. The poor in less developed countries are making their voices heard in liberation movements and popular front organizations. The demand is for greater popular power or participation, and this demand is not easily reconciled with the requirements of modern technological systems.

In sum, the technological process, while it produces mountains of goods to consume, an improved quality of material living, and new forms of interaction, narrows participation and threatens responsibility and freedom. The result is paradoxical. The opportunities for controlling nature and society, for interaction on a global scale, and for the exercise of wide-ranging freedoms—provided they are affordable—are everywhere increasing. At the same time, there is a widespread sense that things are out of control and that human beings are less and less masters of the technological process they have created. Technical systems and bureaucratic organizations seem to grow as if they had a life of their own. Bigness and complexity swamp smallness and simplicity. Decisions vital to the community are made without conscious awareness by impersonal and difficult-to-pinpoint "forces." The ability to respond to these "forces" decreases for want of competence. Dependency on specialized experts who themselves are incompetent in areas outside their own is increased.

Understanding the Problem

Mike Mulligan experienced these "forces," but he did not comprehend what was going on. He passively responded to the market, happy when it provided work on the great construction projects, sad when it declared Mary Anne obsolete. Mike was not alone then, nor is he now. Today North Americans encounter the latest edition of these forces in the computer revolution and are equally perplexed. What is it that has brought the technological process to such a dominant place in the culture of developed countries and threatens to do the same in less developed countries?

To get at this question several things bear mentioning, first in summary, then individually in greater detail. The dramatic convergence of economic and technological forces with new ideas and values, a convergence which occurred first in Western Europe and has now spread throughout the world, is the starting point. This convergence led to the gradual development of a way of life in which science-based technology is the most powerful social force. This way of life imposes certain forms on societies and cultures with which it comes in contact. People adapt themselves, or in what is called *reverse adaptation*, are adapted to it. The values and ways which lead to its perpetuation become their values and ways. Certain groups push and give limited direction to this way of life and are disproportionately served by its perpetuation. These groups are made up of individuals who by themselves are unimportant to the system. Individuals are interchangeable in its processes and have little control over outcomes beyond their own area of specialized knowledge. It is a narrow way of life in terms of participation and spirituality. This narrowness is the source of consequences, many of which run counter to basic Christian principles.

To unpack this condensed summary of the "forces" that affected Mike and Mary Anne, and now every person in the world, the place to start is with the historical convergence of economic and technological forces with new ideas and values that occurred first in Western Europe.

1. *Historical convergence and dominance.* Sociologists refer to the type of society found in Western Europe in the Middle Ages as a "traditional society." Such a society is traditional because of the importance for survival of maintaining an unchanging social order. The dominant grouping in a traditional society is generally the close-knit family or clan. Such a society is decentralized, homogeneous, and has fixed occupational patterns. Religious or quasi-religious ideological systems dominate it. Technological innovation and commercial activity are not virtues.

For reasons that are not altogether clear even now, a way of life with tremendous power was born in the traditional society of Western Europe. It slowly revolutionized the society which gave it birth and finally, with gathering momentum, moved out to become a powerful worldwide force.

Historians and social scientists have been able to piece together some of the forces which converged to produce this way of life in the late 17th century.[6] These include: 1) the optimism of the Renaissance and its emphasis on the human in contrast to the divine; 2) population increase; 3) the fruition of a long technical experience and new scientific discoveries which, in addition to providing new knowledge, called traditional church authority into question; 4) the availability of Arabic advances in science and technology; 5) the voyages of discovery and the influx of gold as a result of exploiting these discoveries; 6) the rise of independent craft guilds and the reemergence of trade; 7) the struggle for social power between a rising middle class and landed aristocrats; 8) Christian beliefs about nature and human dominance over it; and 9) certain ideas and values emerging from the Protestant Reformation.

What is amazing is the convergence of so many different forces. It was a unique convergence which provided new outlets for the human will to power and partially satisfied age-old desires to improve material standards. In the 18th century the process of change from traditional to modern picked up steam literally and figuratively. The marriage of science and technology in England, often symbolized by Watt's steam engine, drew together the early stages. Up to that time, science and technology had been separate endeavors, the former the preserve of intellectual aristocrats, the latter left to artisans. After this marriage it was appropriate to speak of science-based technology and the technological process.

Equally important was another marriage, that between capitalism and ideas emerging from the Protestant Reformation. This convergence of material forces and religion-based ideas was first discussed by German sociologist Max Weber early in this century.[7] Weber outlined the consequences of certain Protestant doctrines on the way Europeans thought and acted. In particular, he stressed the significance of Calvinism, perhaps best exemplified in America by Puritanism, with its single-minded devotion to what it took to be the will of God. "Serve God in everything you do," might just as well have been the Calvinist motto, and service meant hard work, the exploitation of nature for human ends, practicality, the rational use of time and energy, honesty, frugality, and individual achievement. Service to God also included the avoidance of idleness and the pleasures of the flesh, so that Weber could say it combined a thrust for more and more money with the avoidance of all spontaneous pleasures. Weber described this religion-based set of values and beliefs as a way of life and called it the Protestant ethic, known more popularly today as the work ethic. It was his view that capitalism and the work ethic mutually reinforced each other, producing an economic system and supporting ideology with amazing vitality.

A system of economic organization, an ideology which soon lost track of its religious roots, and the combined forces of science and technology were the most important factors leading to the production of goods and services at an ever-quickening pace. Rising material standards were dubbed "progressive," and this title rubbed off on all elements of the process. Above all this process granted power—power over nature, over people, and seemingly over human destiny itself.

2. *The domination of technical systems.* This power is awesome. It seems to extend human mastery and control in all directions. The prevailing view sees it as a means to human ends consciously chosen by individuals and groups with definite purposes in mind. Underlying this view, according to political scientist Langdon Winner, are three assumptions:

1. That men know best what they themselves have made;
2. That the things men make are under their firm control;
3. That technology is essentially neutral, a means to an end; the benefit or harm it brings depends on how men use it.[8]

Also in this view the problem of participation in community and the erosion of certain freedoms and responsibilities is seen as a consequence of misuse. People do not need to be separated by canals. Bridge technologies are available to counter this negative side effect. Mary Anne's fate in the junk heap is not predetermined. She can be and indeed was converted into the heating plant for the Popperville town hall. To include the voice of the people affected by a given technology, the process need only be expanded in terms of planning.

This view of mastery and control, with the companion views of the essential neutrality of the technological process and problems as mere side effects, still dominates popular perceptions. Running counter to it is another view which takes several forms.

Common to these forms is the question of control. Does Mike Mulligan really control his situation? Or does the way in which he has organized his life and sold his services dictate his way of life and thinking, thus effectively eliminating further choice? Does the use of modern technology require a certain way of life and certain values of Mike so that the range of his choices is narrowed to one way and one set of values no matter what he may prefer? Or is it that a new group of political masters has wrestled control away from Mike and is now manipulating him to its own ends?

One perspective which seriously questions Mike's control of the situation holds that the way men and women organize their productive lives determines, or at least is the single most important factor influencing, the way they live and the values they hold.[9] So in a simple society where some are hunters, others are gatherers, and still others perform domestic chores, there is a relatively simple division of labor, smaller, more homogeneous groupings, and a value system which supports the various roles and enforces tradition. Politically, a tribal system is the usual form.

As the organization of production becomes more complex and the web of interactions increases, so the social system becomes more complex. Values which were appropriate to the simpler hunting and gathering mode no longer fit. New values and new political forms supportive of the new form of production emerge and come to dominate. Social change comes about through changes first occurring in productive processes. As new productive processes prove more efficient, so the values and political systems change to support them.

In this view Mary Anne, a steam shovel, is just one stage in the evolution of productive forces from primitive tools to giant earth-moving machines and beyond. She has her day in the sun and Mike's values support her, but when more powerful shovels are introduced, Mike's values and Mary Anne become obsolete. Mike and Mary Anne, according to this perspective, stand somewhere in the chain between the simple, close-knit, and more personal traditional arrangement and the complex, pluralistic, and impersonal ways of modern technological society. They have no control over the evolutionary forces and very little over their own destiny.

In some extreme forms this perspective becomes a full-blown

determinism. Each generation is said to be determined, or at
least strongly conditioned, by a social and technical inheritance
that it does not choose. For the most part this inheritance must
simply be accepted as given and usually is. The function of educational institutions is to make the Mike Mulligans of the world
feel at home with their inheritance, or, as Karl Marx would have
said, their chains.

In less extreme forms the dominant influence of technology
and the social organization associated with it is said to be characteristic only of this particular era, and no attempt is made to
draw general lessons of history or to rule out some limited range
of free choice. The fear is expressed, however, that freedom and
participation are gradually eroding as the technological process
comes to dominate.

In a variation of this perspective, mastery and control are combined with a limited determinism. In this variation technological
domination is something human beings "drift" into, not a law-
bounded process guided to an inevitable conclusion.[10] Individuals
and groups acting within a narrow range make technological
choices largely on the basis of economic criteria. Thousands of
these choices are made every day. The problem emerges with the
discovery that all the choices taken together produce an outcome
which cannot be predicted from the choices themselves. The
whole is different from the sum of its parts. According to Langdon Winner:

> A multiplicity of technologies, developed and applied under
> a very narrow range of considerations, act and interact in
> countless ways beyond the anticipations of any person or insti-
> tution. Except in cases of extreme danger or disaster, there are
> almost no existing means for controlling or regulating the
> products in this chain of events. People still retain their logical
> position as users and controllers of technology. But in the
> broader context which transcends "use" and "control," this
> logic is of little consolation. As the speed and extent of tech-
> nological innovations increase, societies face the distinct possi-
> bility of going adrift in the vast sea of "unintended conse-
> quences." [11]

Examples in support of this variation of the perspective
abound. The automobile is perhaps the most obvious, with its
tremendous impact on social customs. The vast social changes

which came with the automobile were not part of Henry Ford's decision to mass-produce the Model T. They were something society drifted into. Today the rapid spread of computer technologies may harbor equally vast changes, and few people are asking what they might be.

3. *Technology imposes certain forms.* Technologies are like babies in the sense that choosing them implies a commitment to support them with whatever is necessary for their proper functioning. Modern technologies have many requirements, and their use imposes certain "imperatives" which cannot be avoided. In addition to these imperatives are what might be called the consequences or effects of technology, that is, the tendency of certain outcomes to recur from the use of a technology.

The logic of the technological imperative is simple:

> The technological imperative contains a logic that accounts for much of the way change occurs in modern society. . . . [I]f you desire X and if you have chosen the appropriate means to X, then you must supply all of the conditions for the means to operate. To put it differently, one must provide not only the means but also the entire set of means to the means. . . . Failure to follow the dictates of the technical imperative has a . . . severe outcome: a device produces no results (or the wrong ones). For this reason, once the original choice has been made, the action must continue until the whole system of means has reached its proper alignment.[12]

Economist John Kenneth Galbraith illustrates the imperative and its consequences by comparing the preparations that went into the building of a Ford in 1903 with those for the Mustang in 1961.[13] The 1903 Ford took approximately six months from conception to market, a capital endowment of $100,000, and 125 men. The Mustang in contrast took three and one-half years, $60 million, and men and women numbering in the tens of thousands. From this contrast Galbraith draws six imperatives of technology.

First, the completion of the task with most modern technologies takes time. Time is required to apply scientific or other organized knowledge to a myriad of practical tasks such as the machining of parts, the selection of steel, and the marketing of the final product. Each step must be carefully and slowly planned so the multiplicity of operations meet in an assembly line pro-

62 Putting on the Brakes

ducing Mustangs to be sold in markets far distant from the manufacturing plant.

Second, the entire operation requires large amounts of capital to pay planners, to build the assembly line, to advertise the product, and to transport the finished product to market.

Third, each task contributing to the final product must be precisely defined. This means division and subdivision of tasks into minute component parts with a resulting inflexibility once decisions are made. To change one part means a host of other parts must be changed to accommodate it.

Fourth, modern technology requires a specialized labor force. It does not necessarily require smarter men and women, although this helps. What it needs is average people trained in narrow specialties corresponding to the subdivision of the task.

Fifth, and a consequence of the fourth, is the need for specialists in organization and management who are essential to the smooth running and final outcome of a very complex enterprise. Management specialists must in turn have authority to coordinate, a requirement which generally imparts a hierarchical pattern of organization.

Sixth, detailed, rational planning must accompany the entire process. This means control and order, not just of the productive process, but, more critically, of markets. $60 million in the early 1960s, now several times that due to inflation, is not a sum the Ford Motor Company wants to risk on fickle markets. Costs must be kept low and potential buyers persuaded to consume. Thus the requirement for planning entails manipulation of suppliers, consumers, and even the political environment to ensure stability and success.

The reason for concern about freedom and participation is implicit in these requirements of modern technological systems. The Mustang demands an ordered environment. Chance, outbreaks of charismatic spirituality, dissidence, and nontechnical creativity are potentially disastrous. Time and space must be ordered. The rich variety of human characteristics must be narrowed to fit special operations and the need for rational planning and control, at least on the job during an inflexible eight-hour period. Men and women without the requisite skills, for example, Mike and Mary Anne or farmhands in developing countries who do not fit the technical requirements of the Green Revolution, become surplus and obsolete. The planning process itself, at least once a basic decision is reached, is closed to further participation. The manipulation resulting from the strict cost accounting and marketing practices needed to ensure profit runs counter to the so-called freedom of choice prized in democratic capitalism.

To Galbraith's list of six imperatives, and in a similar vein, Langdon Winner adds several attributes or tendencies of modern technological systems and notes their consequences.[14] To start with, he points out that the material world created by modern technological systems is artificial. This artificial restructuring involves both nature and society. Synthetic materials such as plastics replace biodegradable materials such as wood. Highly mobile and densely populated communities replace groupings based on the agricultural cycle. One consequence of this artificiality, according to Winner, is that human beings find themselves responsible for an increasing share of worldly conditions and must continually attend to the maintenance of the system they have created. Another consequence is the breakup of traditional communities, where each person had a place and a sense of participation was more or less guaranteed.

Winner calls his second attribute *extension*. Modern technologies extend human capability and grant to those who control them vast new powers with no instructions on participative use. Dangerously, they allow for control through remote channels. Increasingly power is being exercised from places far from local communities like Popperville, which in traditional societies were the primary centers of power, and by people whose interests are economic growth and profit. This remoteness and alien control adds to the sense of powerlessness and lack of participation.

The third attribute is the increasing dominance of human thinking by a certain mode of rationality. Proof by the test of sense, a linear mode of thought, systematic arrangement, detailed organization of minute tasks, and above all, the quest for efficiency in all aspects of life are the hallmarks of this rationality. Admittedly this form of rationality replaced an even narrower rationality based on tradition. It also opened up vast new areas for exploration. But these admissions do not lessen its narrowness. Nor do they help to include those who do not think along its lines.

Winner's fourth attribute was implied by Galbraith. Modern technologies are large-scale, resource- and energy-intensive sys-

tems necessitating huge inputs of capital and labor. The superhighways, airports, rail systems, and canals Mike and Mary Anne
built all dwarf Popperville with its small-scale, localized way of
doing things. Increasing scale is usually attributed to the complexity of modern technology and to economies derived from
size. Small-scale and simple technologies produced in local indus-
tries by a few people are, of course, imaginable and do exist. The
dominant trend, however, is toward larger size and greater complexity, if not in the technologies themselves at least in the organizations that produce them. The problem for participation is
obvious. Large size and complexity overwhelm all but the most
intrepid. Mike and Mary Anne are easily pushed aside by the
newer and bigger shovels.

With his fifth attribute Winner observes that modern technologies are enmeshed in a web of interconnected and inter-
dependent components. The tendency is to view the components
as equal and to celebrate the increased participation created by
the web. This view is distorted, insists Winner. It is like saying
that an individual and the phone company are equally and mutually dependent, when in fact the partners are vastly unequal in
power. The phone company is able to cut off the relationship
with little or no adverse consequences. For the individual the
consequences are far more serious.

As for participation, a great number of superficial relationships and minor dependencies are hardly a substitute for in-depth
encounters and a voice in decisions. It is the quality and depth
of relationships, not the quantity, which make for participative
communities. In fact, claims Winner, the use of modern technologies tends to create a vast number of dependencies on large,
hierarchical organizations which are not reciprocally dependent.
This contributes to the perceived feelings of powerlessness, lack
of participation, and loss of control.

Winner's sixth attribute, central control, is also related to several of Galbraith's imperatives. Central control as a requirement
resulted from the need to coordinate diverse operations in a large-
scale network and to centralize power to protect and extend investments. Autonomous action is truly possible only at the center.
The implications of this for participation are obvious. Centralized control which does not allow for autonomy on the periphery
is the antithesis of participation. It leads to the manipulation of
people without their consent.

Finally Winner argues that modern technological systems are vulnerable to severe breakdown. Winner cites the East Coast blackout of 1965. He might have also mentioned Three Mile Island or nuclear war. The consequence of this attribute is a moral imperative that major systems be kept in constant working order and carefully guarded. So we have come full circle. Modern technology, like a baby, demands attention and protection, far more than the less sophisticated technologies of earlier periods.

In summary, to say the use of modern technologies involves a free act of mastery on the part of its designers and managers and that technologies themselves are neutral is misleading. Galbraith's imperatives and Winner's attributes render such a view simplistic. Technologies are not neutral. They, or at least the process which incorporates them, impose certain conditions and are a powerful force in determining the direction of post-industrial society.

4. *People adapt themselves to or are adapted by the technological process.* If modern technological processes impose certain forms and have negative side effects such as the obsolescence of Mike and Mary Anne, then North Americans seem more than willing to accept these forms and not worry overly much about the side effects. The view of mastery and control, with its central belief in the progressive nature of modern technology, is still potent.

Increasingly, however, critics are being heard. One of the strongest has been Jacques Ellul.[15] For Ellul the adoption of modern technologies has brought a form of slavery that is far more than mere "side effects." Not only do technologies impose requirements, but economic and technological ends become human ends, and humans in the process become means. Mastery and control are reversed. Human organizations are tailored to fit technologies. Development strategies are put to work which fit the requirements of existing technologies, not the needs of the poor.

The end result, according to Ellul, is that all but the most sensitive get caught up in the web of technological society with pathological completeness, either adapting themselves or being adapted to its processes. One way adaptation occurs is through the superior capacity of modern technologies to fulfill basic physical needs. Given the age-old fight against scarcity, whatever is able to improve material standards of living exerts a powerful influence, even if the price is dependency and reduced participation. Swiss historian of architecture Siegfried Giedion offers the trivial but illustrative example of the bath and its social role. Bathing historically, he points out, served a social function. Public baths in many societies were a place to congregate and share news.

> This century, in the time of full mechanization, created the bath-cell, which, with its complex plumbing, enameled tub, and chromium taps, is appended to the bedroom. This arrangement, of course, has no thought of bathing as a social institution or a means of regeneration. A period like ours, which has allowed itself to become dominated by production, finds no time in its rhythms for institutions of this kind.[16]

Adaptation is also made possible because so many modern technologies overwhelm us with their size and complexity. Trying to understand what goes into a jet plane, to wade through the volumes of regulations governing the airline industry, or even to make it through O'Hare Field is too much for the uninitiated. It is easier to acquiesce and climb on the airplane.

Still another way adaptation occurs is through what is learned and the language used in learning. Much of the American educational system is oriented to occupational success. Education into a particular occupation predisposes students to accept as natural the organization of that occupation and its ways of thinking. Adaptation comes easily in small subtle ways. No propaganda is necessary. The way that is conducive to the spread of modern technology and the consumer goods it produces becomes a way of life.

This way of life is reinforced by the use of certain words. Individuals are asked for "feedback" instead of participation. "Progress" is equated with economic and technological expansion. Systems language becomes the norm in the social sciences. Jargon peculiar to narrow specialization is rife.

The end note in all this is what might be called *reserve adaptation*, which Langdon Winner defines as "the adjustment of human ends to match the character of available means." [17] In Winner's view, persons adapt themselves not only to the order, discipline, and pace of modern organizations, but also come to accept the values and beliefs conducive to technical processes as central to their lives as a whole. "Efficiency, speed, precise man-

agement, rationality, productivity, and technical improvement
become ends in themselves applied obsessively to areas of life
in which they would previously have been rejected as inappropriate." Human needs get translated into material objects.

> Abstract general ends—health, safety, comfort, nutrition, shel-
> ter, mobility, happiness, and so forth—become highly instru-
> ment specific. The desire to move about becomes the desire to
> possess an automobile; the need to communicate becomes the
> necessity of having telephone service; the need to eat becomes
> the need for a refrigerator, stove, and convenient supermarket.
> Implied here also is the requirement that the whole chain of
> techniques and instruments which satisfies each need is well
> constructed and maintained.[18]

5. *Who controls?* The question of control engenders as much
emotion now as it did over 100 years ago when Karl Marx first
raised the issue for industrial society. Three positions on this
question stand out. There are those who with Jacques Ellul say
that the technological process itself is in control and adapts human beings to its requirements. Participation is essentially nonexistent. There are others, usually Marxists, who argue that the
technological process is firmly in the hands of its owners. According to their view, modern technological organization and its
attendant value system is another in a long line of slaveries by
means of which a dominant class forces subservient classes to
pay for its play. Participation is not allowed.

There are still others like Langdon Winner who hold that the
technological process, the side effects of modern technology, and
adaptation are matters of drift. Limited control is exerted by
individuals and groups devising and implementing specific technologies within a narrow context, but the totality of techniques
is without control and drifts along unattended.

Short of deciding which of these positions is correct, a few
conclusions can be drawn. First, technological systems are not
people, in spite of the tendency to personify them as with Mary
Anne and her emotions. Second, human beings devise and implement specific technologies. There is a range of choice at this
level. Third, a relatively few individuals and groups perform
the tasks of devising and implementing. Fourth, the rewards
for devising and implementing are substantial and flow disproportionately to the owners and managers of modern tech-

nology. Fifth, modern technologies yield power, and, as with the rewards, power is disproportionately in the hands of the owners and directors. Sixth, there is a quality to the whole, to the ensemble of all techniques as Ellul would call it, that gives the appearance of uncontrolled drift and reverse adaptation. Seventh and last, getting a hold on this ensemble of techniques will be the most difficult task of all, not only because its dynamics are little understood, but also because its immensity and complexity may well be beyond control. Indeed, to take control involves an ironical twist. The irony comes in using still more techniques to deal with techniques. The commitment to the technological way of life is only increased.

Conclusion

Participation is a difficult commodity to come by because it is not a commodity. Deep down it is something that happens between people when they are not governed by the laws of commodities, that is, the laws of buying and selling, supply and demand, and profit making. No wonder it is such a precious thing both in the United States and throughout the world where buying and selling occupy so many. Participation is freely sharing in decisions. It is joining and contributing to the processes that affect one's life. It is having a place to come home to where you can be yourself and share in a community that knows and cares for you.

In so many ways modern technological systems close off participation and hence freedom and responsibility. In the countries where pretechnical traditions still hold sway, it threatens to introduce new ways with great power. What is gained is the power of material things. What is threatened is the power of tradition and the spirit of a people. In societies already dominated by economic and technological expansion, participation in decisions, in communities, and in nature struggles to stay alive. Fortunately the spirit is unquenchable, and some forms of technology actually are compatible with and foster the expression of the spirit. Still, it is an uneven struggle. Technological systems produce things which delight the imagination. If not the delight over consumption goods, then certainly the health gains, the increased mobility, and the better selectivity make for a consuming way of life beyond which the Word of God is often hard to hear.

The dilemma raised by modern technology is profound and deep. Not to use a given technology is to give up the benefits it offers. Few people weigh the costs of each and every decision to utilize available technologies. The benefits are obvious and the costs subtle and seemingly abstract. But to get deeply involved in the consumption of modern technologies and the society which supports them means running the risk of a narrowing commitment which tends to cut off participation. To control the ensemble of techniques—that uncontrolled totality of specific technologies, institutions, values, and beliefs—with an eye to reconceiving the ensemble and directing specific technologies to higher ends, is to enter into the paradox that control itself is part of the ensemble. It is the dilemma of the sorcerer's apprentice.

For those in traditional societies there is still some hope that the technological process can be held at arm's length, appropriated where it fits local conditions and improves material standards, rejected where it does not. Perhaps some combination of modern technology and tradition leading to self-reliant development is possible.

For those in developed countries, such as the United States, the task is both easier and harder. It is easier because the conditions of poverty are not so all-consuming, harder because so much has already been invested in present ways of living. Somehow in this situation the spirit of participation in decisions, in community, and in nature must be recovered. Is it too naive to expect that Christianity can be the wellspring of recovery? Does Christianity have anything of value to say about size, community, and the dangers of material possessions?

CHAPTER 4

Limits to Growth
and Sustainability

The third problem, and the one causing the most anxiety to North Americans, is that of limits to economic and technological growth.[1] The anxiety arises from a legitimate fear that high population growth rates, the exhaustion of energy and resource stocks, and pollution of the environment will result in reduced standards of living and maybe even severe shortages. To those who have applied brakes to their assumptions and are pausing at the end of the superhighway, this problem is forcing decisions, not just about the sustainability of present living standards, but about justice and participation.

On the one hand they are aware of the many drivers still racing along the superhighway as if there were no changes in assumptions, no limits to material abundance, and no decisions about direction required. Considering the mammoth social change a shift of attitudes and actions would require, perhaps, they conclude, it would be better to pursue the superhighway of growth in hopes that new technologies will continue to extend the dual lanes to each new horizon. Or if not this, they see the pictures of Mike Mulligan proudly digging and scrapping his way to happiness through hard work on giant construction projects. Is there not something to be proud of in all this building even if it may involve a "Tower of Babel" mentality?

Or finally, they hear certain voices: the voices of the poor demanding justice and a share of the new building projects; the voices of the technological optimists who regard talk about limits as cries of "wolf"; and the voices of the economists who say prices will signal when to put on the brakes. Are there really limits to growth? If so, are there not ways around them other than wrenching social change?

On the other hand, they share the anxiety North Americans have about abundance. They note that others of like mind have put on their brakes and are pausing at the same forks in the road. Some have even begun to press on into new ways of living without car or camper. Perhaps change is not so difficult after all. As for Mike Mulligan, maybe there are other roads to satisfaction than through building and consuming in conventional ways. Might another possibility be a way of living based on sharing and sufficiency? And what is the real picture with the poor? Did not the study of poverty and malnutrition reveal that some forms of economic growth and modern technology are actually making things worse in some cases in spite of the celebrated "trickle down" effect? Is growth really all it is claimed to be?

They hear other voices as well: the voices calling attention to the sheer numbers involved in perpetuating growth; the 600 to 700 percent increase in production required to bring the rest of the world to North American consumption levels; [2] the illogic of infinite growth in a finite world; the carbon dioxide and heat pollution which might be caused with production levels of the magnitude envisioned. They also hear the voices of those who are not so optimistic about modern technology. Some even have the audacity to suggest that the technological process itself is limited or creates more problems than it solves. They hear still other voices, which claim that the pursuit of growth will have predictable costs in terms of lost traditions, spirituality, and participation.

Central to their calculations are two interrelated questions, one a factual question, the other a value question. The factual question has to do with the predictability of limits and the need for more sustainable modes. Are there actually physical limits to the expansion of the food supply, to the consumption of energy and resources, and to the pollution absorption capacity of the earth? If not physical limits, are there not social limits which will eventually bring growth to a halt, such as inflation

and the capacities to manage complex systems and to maintain
social order? And beyond these calculations there is the critically
important question of when limits will occur. Are we close to
them or far away? If close, is drastic action necessary? If far
away, can we afford a more leisurely pace?

The problem with answering these factual questions is obvious.
The future involves an element of unpredictability which makes
all but a few lucky guesses seem incredibly naive in retrospect.
In the late 19th century, for example, some urban dwellers were
deeply concerned about the increasing accumulation of manure
in the city streets. Some predicted they would be buried in it if
the growth rate continued. Needless to say the automobile came
to the rescue making their concern seem trivial. But will new
inventions always be forthcoming? Economist Kenneth Boulding
has a few doubts:

> [I]n the last 100 or 200 years we have been extraordinarily
> lucky in finding . . . new and convenient sources of energy and
> materials. We know they are a limited stock and that the
> known stocks at present will be used up in a relatively short
> time. Then the question arises: How likely are we to be that
> lucky twice and so find new and unsuspected sources of energy
> and materials, at present unknown or perhaps even unguessed
> at?[3]

Fortunately the future is not all a matter of guesswork. The
future is in part predictable because it is tied to the present and
past. By extending present trends, some of which will hold, at
least the most outlandish forecasts can be ruled out. Alternative
scenarios are available which take into account some of the vari-
ables. Such scenario building is important because it allows
present decision-makers to make at least partially informed pro-
jections and to reduce guesswork.

Given this element of unpredictability, gauging the future is
fertile ground for both fools and experts to plant their own self-
interest and cherished values. This is why the first question
about facts and the second about values are interrelated, and
those who are pausing at the end of the superhighway need to
exercise caution. Forecasts of the future are never totally objective or interest free. Thus the second question, that of which
future is desirable, must be taken into account. This question
of desirability includes a consideration of basic values and self-

interest. The debate over growth reveals a not-so-remarkable co-
incidence between occupation and the sort of future one predicts.
Economists, business executives, and technologists, with the exception of mavericks, are remarkably united in their desire to see
the superhighway continue. Generally, they are also optimistic
about technological fixes and tend to minimize side effects. Con-
versely, counterculture types, Audubon Society members, clergy,
and teachers in the humanities often find themselves in the
opposite ranks.

For Christians the desirability question needs to be asked
using Christian norms and insights. This is the task of the
chapters that follow. For now it is important to recognize that
value orientation is one important factor influencing judgments
on economic growth and technology. The warning that follows
from this insight is to beware of assessments and forecasts of the
future that hide value judgments and self-interest behind sup-
posedly factual analysis.

Limits to Growth

The term *limits to growth* is a misnomer, for it suggests an
end to all forms of growth. Obviously certain forms of growth
can continue, even many forms of economic growth. The forms
of growth which show the greatest signs of limits are: 1) food
and population; 2) pollution; 3) energy and natural resources;
and 4) the social capability to conceive and manage new technologies. To the discussion of these forms must be added a fifth
category: self-limitation, a conscious calculation to limit growth
on the basis of values or because of increasingly expensive trade-
offs.

1. *Population and food.* In the short run there is plenty of
food to go around. Population and food are not the immediate
problem, distribution is. In the long range the picture is different. This is why eliminating grinding poverty now and a
more just distribution are so crucial. Without economic security
and social justice, birth rates will remain high and population
will grow in poorer countries. In the long run, barring unfore-
seen breakthroughs in food production and maybe even with
them, starvation is inevitable unless population growth rates are
drastically reduced.

Approximately 4.5 billion people now inhabit the earth, a

figure which is growing at an annual rate of 1.7%. This growth rate produces a doubling of the population every 40 years. How many more doublings can be sustained depends on new technologies, the capacity for justice, and human toleration of crowdedness. One thing is sure, however, population growth cannot continue forever.

In most developed countries birth rates are already near replacement levels. Even so, the per capita consumption of food, which is four to five times higher than in the poorest countries, places a much heavier burden on the existing food supply.

Limits to the food supply are not so obvious. Food production is increasing at a rate of 2.3% per year in the United States and at about half that rate in many poor countries. But these numerical increases mask the distributional problem considered in Chapter 2. Furthermore, there is good reason to doubt they are sustainable beyond the turn of the century. The limiting factors are many, and ways around them are not easy to find. Land availability is one limiting factor. Of the 40% of the earth's total land capable of production only about 25%, or one-tenth of the total land, is cultivatable with existing technologies.[4] This percentage could be increased with irrigation but, on the large scale needed, only with massive desalination projects which themselves are dependent on new and cheaper energy technologies. Bringing tropical land into production would also raise this percentage, but this is a risky undertaking because of poor soil and the possibility of adverse climatic and ecological consequences.

If prospects for increasing the amount of land in cultivation are not good, then productivity gains offer some hope. The green revolution has demonstrated that gains are possible under certain conditions. Those gains are the basis of hope in the short, but not necessarily in the long, range where genetic limits to the productivity of plants come into play. Moreover, the green revolution, as we saw in Chapter 2, is expensive, requires huge energy and water inputs, and involves the use of fertilizer, herbicides, and pesticides, none of which are applied without ecological and social side effects.

It is clear that population and probably food production will stabilize either because men and women choose to stabilize them or because of natural necessity. What remains in doubt is the amount of time available until the limiting factors take effect.

2. *Pollution.* Of the several potential limits, the earth's pollution absorption capacity is the least pressing. With a combination of capital investment, technological innovation, and changed attitudes about wastes, the threat of this limit is already lessening. To say this is neither to minimize the current costs of pollution nor to deny the existence of severe pollution problems. Nor is it to say that basic ecological support systems have an unlimited capacity to absorb pollution.

The types of pollution are familiar enough: water pollution from animal and industrial wastes; air pollution from manufacturing processes and the burning of fossil fuels; radiation pollution from nuclear accidents and waste storage; heat pollution from combustion and the so-called greenhouse effect; and less serious in terms of limits but still bothersome, noise and visual pollution. Some types of pollution, for example, mercury, cadmium, lead, and asbestos, are extremely serious health hazards. Their use and release into ecological systems is strictly controlled. Nuclear radiation has known effects on all living organisms. The dumping of chemical wastes, as Hooker Chemical did in Love Canal, can have drastic local consequences.

Perhaps the most worrisome and least understood are the climatic effects of pollution. Carbon dioxide released into the atmosphere in the burning of fossil fuels acts like a blanket producing a greenhouse or warming effect. The severity of this problem or whether it is even a problem is not yet clear. The oceans are capable of absorbing significant amounts of carbon dioxide, and particulate matter suspended in the air by the same combustion processes blocks some of the sun's heat from reaching the earth. The net result may be a balancing of the two effects. But should the earth's atmosphere warm even a few degrees, the release of water stored in polar ice caps would inundate coastal cities and eliminate farm land.

Pollution control is costly and can dampen productivity. With most forms of pollution, monetary and energy costs increase dramatically with increased levels of control. A control level of 50% is usually possible with modest expenditures. Even levels of 80 to 90% are sometimes within reasonable cost. Beyond these levels, however, rapidly escalating costs are encountered. As a consequence, polluters are often allowed to operate with only partial control. Thus the potential exists for pollution absorption capacity to be reached through increased production, even though fairly effective measures are being taken on individual sources of pollution. Still there is a gain, for absorption capacity will be reached at a much later time.

Pollution absorption capacity itself is an elusive concept. Capacity depends on specific ecological systems. Some systems are extremely fragile at key points, others more resistant. Water and air are capable of absorbing and scrubbing vast quantities of pollution, but the systems that depend on them are seldom as resistant. Absolute levels above which a system is destroyed exist for most organisms, but this level is seldom reached at once by all parts of the system. Thus the relevant question is not always the destruction of entire species, but how many human, animal, and plant lives are pollution-intensive production and consumption worth. Unfortunately this trade-off between life and consumption is seldom made explicit. Consumption decisions are not linked to the possibility of cancer 20 years in the future.

Most North Americans would like to have it both ways—good health and high levels of consumption. This combination may be possible but not without huge expenditures of money for pollution control and large doses of energy to maintain production levels. Money spent on pollution control means money diverted from other investments. In principle, pollution control and economic growth are compatible. Whether pollution control slows economic growth depends on where the money comes from to finance it. If investments in more efficient processes are cut to finance pollution control, then growth slows. If, however, control is financed by cutting the military budget or unessential consumption, then growth-producing investments may continue.[5] In addition, pollution control is costly in terms of energy. The most obvious example is the automobile. Emission control devices reduce gasoline mileage.

To maintain or increase consumption levels, large doses of energy will also be required. Increased production does not necessarily mean more pollution. Conservation, more efficient production methods, and less pollution-intensive forms of energy could allow more production with the same or less amount of energy. But this is not the case in the short run and perhaps not on the scale needed to keep production levels increasing. Advocates of growth will call on coal and nuclear energy to sustain and increase production. Both pose serious environmental risks.

The relation between energy and pollution points to the overall interrelatedness of problems, "Limits to growth" is not many individual problems lumped under a single heading. Questions about pollution, energy, food production, and technology are interwoven so that decisions in one area have an impact in all others. Perhaps the best example of this is the close relation between technology and pollution which environmentalist Barry Commoner has persuasively demonstrated. According to Commoner the single most important cause of environmental pollution in the post-World War II period is the host of new technologies at the heart of North American affluence; for example, nonreturnable bottles, synthetic fibers, air conditioners, plastics, and nitrogen fertilizers.[6] Commoner concludes:

> The overall evidence seems clear. The chief reason for the environmental crisis that has engulfed the United States in recent years is the sweeping transformation of productive technology since World War II. The economy has grown enough to give the United States population about the same amount of basic goods, per capita, as it did in 1946. However, productive technologies with intense impacts on the environment have displaced less destructive ones. The environmental crisis is the inevitable result of this counter-ecological pattern of growth.[7]

3. *Energy and natural resources.* The era of cheap, abundant energy and natural resources is over. The end of the era was signaled by the dramatic rise in energy prices during the 1970s. This rise in prices reflected several underlying instabilities which together seriously threaten economic expansion. The immediate cause of rising prices was the newfound power of a few oil-rich nations, in particular Saudi Arabia. The ability of these nations to exact higher prices for petroleum was a consequence of their effective control of supply in a period of increasing demand and a lack of substitutes in the short range.

Behind this immediate cause lurks a larger problem. Still cheap relative to many potential substitutes, and having the property of easy storage, supplies of oil and gas are finite and exhaustible. How long they will continue to serve as major fuels is an open question, due to the speculative and price-sensitive character of reserves and the impossibility of predicting the costs of substitutes. The nearly unanimous opinion, however, is that

at current usage rates both oil and gas will be in short supply
sometime in the next century and remaining supplies will be
very expensive. Increased consumption will, of course, reduce
the time it takes for supplies to become scarce and expensive.
It will also lead to further dependency on the oil-rich nations
and on the corporations and technical people who produce the
oil.

Reserves will be dramatically increased if the oil locked up in
shale and tar sands can be tapped at a reasonable cost. Current
technologies are not cost competitive and have the drawback
of being environmentally destructive. Several corporations, Oc-
cidental Petroleum for one, are experimenting with new, less
environmentally destructive technologies, but the cost of production is still far higher than available alternatives.

Coal has also been a major source of energy for industrial
expansion. There are sufficient coal reserves to last several hundred years even with expanded consumption. Located mostly
in already-developed countries with more than three-quarters
of known reserves being in the United States, the Soviet Union,
Europe, and China, coal is not a cheap and plentiful source
for less-developed countries. Of great concern are the serious
drawbacks to increased consumption, notably the dangers and
environmental degradation associated with mining, the cost of
transportation, and the pollution caused by combustion. From
an environmental perspective coal is no bargain and may well
be more problematic than nuclear energy.

Nuclear energy has a far worse reputation, however. Once the
bright hope for the future, it is now so bedeviled with problems
that new orders have ceased in the United States. The problems
are well known: limited supplies of uranium, radiation, accidents such as Three Mile Island, waste storage, time delays, high
costs, the threat of nuclear proliferation, vulnerability to sabo-
tage, and the large scale and complexity of the technology. The
most limiting factor at present is cost, but this only reflects efforts
to solve the other problems. The price of nuclear energy per
kilowatt hour of electricity has increased in recent years faster
than competing sources of energy. Proponents of nuclear energy
still see it, however, as a major transitional fuel and hope that
research leading to reasonably priced breeder and fusion reactors
will extend fuel supplies at an acceptable cost to the environment.

Hopes for fusion are not particularly great. Fusion reactions, as for example in the hydrogen bomb or in the sun, release tremendous quantities of energy but only at extremely high temperatures. In comparison to fission reactions there is less radiation and greatly reduced problems with waste storage. The difficulty comes in trying to harness the reaction. No known substance can contain the extremely high temperatures. Experiments with laser beams and magnetic fields offer some promise, but successful containment is still far off.

Solar power in its many forms offers interesting possibilities. Photovoltaic cells which convert sunlight directly into electricity are currently being used on spaceships, but the electricity they produce is approximately five times as expensive as the cheapest alternative. In some passive forms, such as collectors on roofs for hot water and space heating, solar is already competitive. Experiments for large-scale use, one of which employs parabolic mirrors to focus the sun's rays on a single location to boil water and generate steam, demonstrate that solar energy technologies can be large scale and centralized as well as small scale and decentralized. The advantage of solar power, however, lies in its possibilities for small, local uses where high temperatures are not necessary. Space heating, a large consumer of energy, offers the greatest number of possibilities.

Solar energy comes in many forms, all renewable. Hydroelectric energy accounts for about 4% of electricity generated in the United States, but most sites have been exploited. Experiments with wind, tides, and ocean thermal gradients show some promise. None of these alone offers potential as a major source, but together they are significant. Wind especially has potential as a source of small, local consumption. Finally there is the source called biomass, which is the conversion of organic matter into energy through the combustion or fermentation of wood and crops, the burning of wastes, and the production of gasohol. Again not a major source for industrial expansion, biomass is renewable and has possibilities for local, small scale use.

Balancing supply calculations are the figures on demand.[8] Total world demand for energy has tripled in the past 25 years. In the same period the demand for oil and gas has multiplied four times and for electricity seven times. In the popular imagination economic expansion and increased supply and demand for

energy go hand in hand. One way to reduce the threat of limits
to energy consumption is to break the connection between economic and energy growth. Conservation is the name given to
efforts aimed at breaking this connection. Some estimates place
the potential savings from conservation as high as 40%.[9] Such
simple things as improved insulation, lower thermostat settings,
more gas efficient automobiles, and energy-efficient buildings are
all effective measures.

Conservation and energy from renewable sources such as solar
are the mainstays of an emerging agreement about energy policy
in the United States. A recent study done at the Harvard Business School, hardly a center for romantic thinking about life-
styles, comes persuasively to this conclusion. The report is quite
explicit: "[T]he nation has only two major alternatives for the
rest of this century—to import more oil or to accelerate the development of conservation and solar energy. . . . Conservation
and solar energy, in our view, are much to be preferred." [10]

The joint energy policy statement of the Presbyterian Church
in the United States is equally explicit:

> In the developed countries change implies a reduction in
> waste, restraint of total energy demand, the decreased con-
> sumption of depletable energy resources, and the prioritizing
> of supplies for basic needs. Also implied is an increase in the
> use of renewable energy resources and improved efficiency.[11]

The agreement on conservation and renewable sources as mainstays includes provision for reduced dependence on fossil fuels, in
particular oil and natural gas. The big problem, of course, is
the transition from oil, natural gas, and other nonrenewable
sources to conservation and renewable sources. This will take
considerable time and means a reorientation of consumption
habits. Coal and nuclear energy usually are proposed as the
transitional fuels for mass consumption. The popularity of nuclear energy is waning rapidly, however. If this trend continues
and the fusion reaction is not quickly harnessed, this leaves coal.
Were coal as clean as it is abundant, a choice would be easy and
the transition to renewable sources smooth. Unfortunately coal
is not clean and its mining is ecologically destructive. These
problems reinforce the need for policies to shorten the time of
the transition to renewable sources through strict conservation.

For the less-developed countries the prospects are similar, but with a great difference. The countries in this category are not large energy consumers. Almost all would like to change this and most have plans for economic development that call for increased energy consumption. If not energy limits, then higher prices threaten to put a crimp in these plans. It is no wonder that critics like C. T. Kurien see talk of limits as a plot by the world's rich to prevent economic development by the world's poor. The question of justice again intrudes and gives added reason for the developed countries to shift to a policy of conservation and renewable sources in order to extend supplies and lower prices.

The question of limited mineral resources is inseparable from that of energy. While a few mineral resources—copper, tin, silver, gold, tungsten, and mercury—have very limited reserves, most minerals are in sufficient supply to last more than a century, given no increase in consumption rates and given abundant, cheap energy. The main problems are keeping consumption at present levels and maintaining abundant, cheap energy. Neither can be assumed. As easy-to-get and rich ore deposits are used up, the energy needed to extract harder-to-get and lower grade mineral resources increases. The increasing demand expected with economic development reduces the time it takes to consume existing reserves. At present growth rates, according to the United States Bureau of Mines, most minerals will be in short supply within a century.[12]

The substitution of synthetic or abundant for scarce minerals is one solution to shortages. There are limits to substitution, however. Substitutable minerals may themselves be in short supply, have inferior properties, or be less efficient. Plastics, often cited as a substitute for various metals, are petrochemicals, and petroleum will be in short supply and increasingly expensive.

Another solution to shortages is the mining of seabeds. Offshore oil drilling is the most obvious example of this, but a potential exists for minerals as well. The extent of this potential is not known. Large deposits of certain minerals, notably manganese, are known to exist in deep seabeds. Current methods of recovery are too expensive to permit exploitation. With rising prices this will probably change, but not in the immediate future.

What is of greater interest at the moment is the recently negotiated Law of the Sea. The Law of the Sea establishes territorial waters, economic zones, rights to oil deposits on continental shelves, and pollution regulations. It also regulates migratory fish, provides for unimpeded passage through narrow straits, and sets up procedures for the settlement of disputes.

Perhaps most significant are its provisions for the mining of seabeds. It establishes a global authority under the auspices of the United Nations with powers to regulate such mining. Included in these provisions is the principle that minerals on the floor of the open sea are part of a "common heritage." What is remarkable about this law is that agreement could be reached by nations with diverse interests. Only four nations have rejected the treaty. One of them, and certainly the most important, is the United States. The Reagan administration has refused its approval because, among other things, it rejects the "common heritage" principle and the provisions which would restrict the freedom of private corporations to exploit the seabed.

The "common heritage" principle is significant. What it implies is a commonality which extends beyond nation-states and in which all nations have the right to participate. It also establishes the rights of poorer nations to a share of the world's minerals even though they do not have the means for recovery. In keeping with the Christian concern for justice and participation, the United States should ratify this law.

While the problems with nonrenewable resources are severe, threats to renewable resources, for example the reduction in sustainable yields of forests, fisheries, and grasslands, are a much more serious matter. Ultimately these are the resources on which life depends. Significantly, their destruction is not independent of how rapidly mineral and energy resources are used up. According to economist Herman Daly:

> [H]igh rates of depletion result in high rates of pollution of air and water which directly threaten biological resources. . . . [M]ore importantly, rapid use of nonrenewables has allowed us to reach and sustain temporarily a combined scale of population and per capita consumption that could not be sustained by renewable resources alone. As these nonrenewable resources run out, the danger is that we will try to maintain the existing scale and rate of growth by overexploiting our renewable resource base.[13]

In summary, high levels of energy and resource consumption will continue to be the way of life of the world's rich minority for some time to come. The reorientation of economies as complex as those found in industrialized societies is a staggering task. Whether or how long such consumption levels can be sustained are questions open to debate. But even if high levels are sustainable, the cost will be great in terms of money, opportunities foregone, and environmental damage.

Ultimately even the factual questions become value questions, for choices must be made regarding which costs to bear. Thus energy choices are social and value choices, however factually they are presented. This must be stressed. If North Americans decide on lives which consume large amounts of energy and resources, they will have elected a society and a value system as well, for only a well-integrated and highly developed system will be able to provide the necessary coordination. The "limits to growth" debate is thus much more than speculation about future material standards of living. At heart it is a conflict about alternative directions for society to take, and the present alternatives, often stated in terms of growth versus sustainability, are radically different.

Those in poorer countries are both better and worse off than those in its richer countries. They are better off because they are already using sustainable methods, however poor they may be. They are worse off because economic improvement is now in doubt and the rich countries seem reluctant to share. From the Christian perspective this is tragic. It calls the rich to reconsider their levels of consumption and waste, to revise their exploitive practices, and to share with the poor. Likewise it calls leaders in the poorer countries to rethink development plans which follow Western patterns.

4. *Social limits.* Impressive as the case for physical limits to certain forms of growth is, many economists, scientists, and business people still agree with a recent Edison Electric Institute study which concluded an assessment of the "limits to growth" thesis with the observation that "there are no absolute limits to man's capacity to adapt and cope with complexity. Given the will to do so, man can devise ever more intricate organization forms and make them work. It is a matter of social choice whether this will be done." [14]

Sociologist Daniel Bell, while agreeing with the Institute that physical limits are not ultimately a threat, thinks its conclusion shows a "lack of appreciation for the complexity of the problem.

It does not allow us to even consider in what way there may or may not be social limits." [15] For Bell the major social limit is the management of increasing scale which necessitates a change in shape of social organization. Bell is skeptical about the ease with which the political will can be mustered for this change.

Social limits take several forms. The first is the many unsolved management problems of modern technological society which "limits to growth" only complicates, notably the old, nagging economic problems of unemployment, inflation, savings, and investment. Piled on top of these "normal" problems is a second social limit, what Barry Commoner claims is a limit to the technological process itself.[16] Commoner argues that technologists necessarily define problems so narrowly and divide them into so many parts that tunnel vision develops. No one has the overview to foresee the many side effects of each technical innovation. The result of this "technological flaw" is an ever-increasing number of unintended stresses which multiply geometrically. The solution, suggests Commoner, is not more "tunnel vision," but a reconception of problems with a view to their full environmental implications, that is, the social management of technology.

Others carry Commoner a step further, maintaining the ills of the unintended outweigh the benefits of the intended.[17] They also stress the inevitability of negative side effects which, if not limiting factors in themselves, are easily made so as opponents take their objections into the political and legal arenas.

Tunnel vision and political opposition are certainly crucial social limits to the technological process. Witness the opposition to nuclear power. There are also problems without technical solution. The outstanding example is population growth. All the new contraceptive technologies in the world will not change the perceived need of the poor that children are an economic necessity. Only a political and ethical solution which puts the poor first will deliver the reform and economic security to change these perceived needs.

Finally, modern technology and growth increase the interaction of people, the interrelations of problems, and the complexity and scale of society. An increase in the interaction of people delays decisions and increases the probability of conflict. The increased interrelation of problems means the increased interrelation of effects, including unintended side effects. Nitro-

69196

gen fertilizer increases farm output, but it depletes petroleum reserves and can be a major source of pollution. Complexity and large scale create power imbalances and a sense of lost control, both of which have political fallout as people seek to regain what they feel they have lost.

This feature of increased complexity and scale points to still another social limit, the limited capacity to manage social systems which Daniel Bell alluded to. Bell believes we face a situation where the scales of function and administrative operation simply do not match, as for example in the hodgepodge of overlapping administrative districts. The consequences are an increase in the costs of providing services and a decrease in efficiency. Behind this lies what he calls "a structure of vested interests that are resistant to change" and which will exert a drag on the social capacity to solve limits problems.[18] Bell is no doubt correct, but in emphasizing the element of vested interests, he overlooks the more difficult administrative task of managing increased complexity, interaction, and interrelation.

5. *Self-limitation.* The limit which may have the greatest impact is really not a limit at all. It is the conscious choice to self-limit. Such a self-limitation is nowhere on the immediate horizon, but a combination of increased social costs, higher prices, changed social values, and increased alarm about technological drift could alter prospects very quickly. The seeds are there. The problems are well known, new values have emerged, and already there is a discernable movement toward conservation. The reduction in gasoline consumption is but one example of what might soon turn into a social choice to consume less energy.

Inevitably this raises the serious question of trade-offs. Would a social choice for sustainability as opposed to the increasing consumption of material goods mean lower levels of consumption and the writing off of the world's poor? The answer is not clear. The advocates of growth claim, of course, that an expanding economy is the only way to relieve poverty and to maintain standards of living.[19] Such an assertion makes sense. Growth has been an important factor in reducing the number of poor in the United States. A closer look, however, reveals questionable assumptions. Growth advocates frequently assume that affluence must be associated with high consumption levels and that poverty is merely the absence of material goods.

In Chapter 2 poverty and malnutrition were seen in part to be a consequence of injustice. Little of what passes for economic growth trickles down to the world's poorest people. In fact, the wrong kinds of growth increase their poverty. Nor does economic growth automatically lead to higher material standards. In accustomed forms it may not even be necessary to make the plight of the world's poorest people significantly better. Agrarian reform which promotes self-sufficiency accomplishes many of the same things.

With regard to affluence, no necessary link exists between heavy consumption and full lives. Granted that Americans have made that linkage. Granted also that there is a level of consumption below which life is miserable. But, with changed attitudes, affluence can be defined in terms of much less consumption. Maintaining excessive material standards does not have to be the paramount social goal.

Sustainability and affluence are not incompatible. With concentration on conservation and renewable resources a fairly high material standard is possible.

The Desirability of Growth

Debates over facts frequently hide incompatible values. Squabbles over the checkbook disguise real problems of marital stress. Battles over local zoning miss the differing economic interests of the protagonists. The debate over growth has much of this quality to it. It is different because the factual question of limits to economic and technological growth is immensely significant in its own right. On its resolution rests the material future of the human race. Concentration on this one question, however, misses the equally important second question of desirability. This second question, while perhaps less consequential, may in fact be the more important in the debate, both in terms of predisposing individuals to one side or the other and determining the road Americans will take to the just, participatory, and sustainable society. In the debate over growth, values and interests play a critical role in assessment of the facts and in setting directions. Given the indeterminancy of the future and the tendency to interpret facts to fit interests, this is not surprising.

Marshalled on the sides of the growth debate are two general groups with a third, more moderate position beginning to emerge.[20] On the one side are those who stoutly maintain that limits to growth are being felt already and will make their full impact within decades. They deny these limits can be avoided by technological "fixes," substitution of plentiful for scarce resources, and massive capital investment. Sometimes heard is the prediction of "overshoot and collapse" unless immediate steps are taken to stabilize population growth and to reduce pollution and the consumption of nonrenewable resources.[21] Eventually, according to this perspective, consumption of material goods in developed countries will be at lower levels either because of ecological destruction, outright shortages, or social choice. The ultimate goal is a "steady-state" or "equilibrium economy" where production levels will depend on the availability of renewable resources and the requirements of ecological support systems. To reach this goal there must be a period of transition in which "appropriate" or "soft" technologies using renewable resources become the norm.

In this view, economic strategies in developed countries should be geared to an immediate reduction in consumption, decentralized structures, and a new appreciation of nature and ecological systems. As for less developed countries, the prospects for development along traditional lines are not good. The best policy is for these countries to scrap development plans which depend on large-scale, energy-intensive technologies and to improve already sustainable modes. Improvements in material standards must come through a slow process concentrating on small-scale, labor-intensive technologies adopted to local systems.

On the other side is the pro-growth position. As an earlier quotation from the Edison Electric Institute Study suggested, advocates of this position have an unbounded faith in technical reason and innovation. "Limits to growth" is nonsense to them, for it places unnecessary governors on the human capacity to find ways around constraints. Some holding this position think the human imagination, working to produce new technologies, will be severely taxed. Others figure limits can be avoided with minor tinkering and fine tuning. Whatever the perceived challenges, advocates of growth agree that the scientists, technologists, and managers behind modern technology are capable of meeting them provided they are given the freedom and resources to do so. They are also favorably disposed to these groups and feel they represent the progressive forces of civilization. Indeed, for most, progress is identified with economic expansion.

Advocates of growth point to the benefits of expansion: the raising of material standards, national power, political stability, and the extra resources growth produces each year to be used for social purposes. The most potent argument ethically is that economic expansion is the only feasible way to reduce poverty and to keep employment levels high.

In their preference for technological solutions, growth proponents are champions of sophisticated and large-scale forms of technology. The social costs of modern technology are minimized as unimportant in themselves or relatively insignificant in comparison to the benefits.

With the sometime exception of those who support growth because it offers the best hope for the poor, most growth advocates are ideologically tuned to many of today's dominant values. Efficiency, productivity, practicality, achievement, and a utilitarian view of nature are just a few of the values characteristically found.

However sketchy, these two characterizations at least give the flavor of the growth debate. What is important is not the thoroughness of the description, but the understanding of social and cultural conflict. Limits to growth is an ideological struggle reflecting deep differences of opinion about where industrialized and traditional societies should be headed. Nowhere is this more evident than in the disagreement over modern technology. One side sees it as a basically benign force and the best hope for human well-being. The other side sees it as out of control. For whatever reason, empirical or ideological, they think or hope limits will force a new direction and thus enable Americans to recover lost values and priorities. "Limits to growth" is thus linked to the discussion in Chapter 3 about technology. Were it not for the factual dimension of the limits debate, it would be just another variant of that discussion. It is also related to the question of poverty and malnourishment in Chapter 2, where the question was the harnessing of technical rationality for service to the world's poor.

Fortunately, bewildered observers of this debate are not left with the either/or of growth or no growth. The World Council of Churches, in its vision of sustainability, provides an alternative. What this means in general terms was stated in Chapter 1. The just, participatory, and sustainable society is not one that rejects economic growth and so-called hard technology. Growth and technology are simply subordinated in the vision to the three values which make up the name.

In the actual discussions there has been a tendency to take the side against large-scale and complex technological solutions and to be skeptical of technical fixes. The popularity of the late British economist E. F. Schumacher and his notion of appropriate technology, and the concept of "soft" technology introduced by Amory Lovins, evidence these tendencies. The tuning of scale to local needs participatively determined seems to be the essence of the World Council position.

In terms of dominant values the World Council discussions have been much closer to the no-growth position. The articulation by a church body of values at variance with those which dominate modern society should come as no surprise. Modern society and the Christian church have different centers, the one in the problem of scarcity, the other in the life and death of Jesus Christ. In this case different centers produce different priorities.

The church proclaims Jesus Christ as the Lord of both the material and spiritual aspects of life. Bringing that lordship to bear on modern society is the purpose of the World Council discussions. Bringing it to bear raises a number of disturbing and painful issues for Christians. To what degree have material consumption and technical virtuosity become ends in themselves divorced from the call of Jesus Christ to serve others and to help the poor? Has the single-minded pursuit of material growth acted like blinders on a horse cutting out the world's poor and ecological systems? Has faith also been a casualty as Americans try to serve two masters? Where is the sense of limits and proportion which proceeds from an understanding of human sin and alienation?

The question of sustainability is forcing decisions about growth, technology, and justice. The options are fairly clear: 1) full speed ahead, problems will be solved; 2) proceed much as before but with minor tinkering: 3) immediate change to a no-growth policy; and 4) the just, participatory, and sustainable society. Each of these options has pitfalls so that it can be said of each that the cure might be worse than the problem. If options 1 and 2 are elected, Christians may find themselves more and more committed to a material way of life. The technologists and the managers who alone can make these options work will have to be paid handsomely for their efforts.

But if the technological cure has its problems, the wrenching change required by options 3 and 4 will not be pleasant. Those options bring fear of the unknown. The necessary economic, political, and value changes are staggering. Robert Heilbroner for one thinks these changes are probably beyond the social capacity of human beings.[22]

However Heilbroner's judgment is assessed, option 4 at least should not be dismissed out of hand. There is movement.[23] Conservation and solar energy are now part of social policy. Gasoline consumption is down. There have been significant gains in pollution control. Environmental protection continues to be a potent political issue.

PART 2

Theological Fuel

CHAPTER 5

Exodus and the Prophets

We now have some knowledge about the three problems which put the brakes on our superhighway assumptions. The time is at hand to start up. First, however, we must fill up the tank and search the map for directions. Our fuel will be biblical theology and our map should reveal the direction of biblical thought on the three problems we have studied.

There are many service stations which offer biblical fuel and maps. Brands, octanes, additives, and maps are available under a variety of names and numbers. Just as there are preferences for different brands and additives, so there are preferences for certain theologies.

Our preference begins by telling a story about a group of slaves in Egypt about 1,250 years before the time of Jesus Christ, a group which without map or direction thought new thoughts about covenants with God. As time passed these new thoughts became old thoughts to the progeny of this group. A group known as prophets emerged and added insight and vitality to the old thoughts. The prophetic interpretation of the covenant was an excellent fuel. It is available even now. Still later something unique was added in the person and work of Jesus Christ. In him God acted decisively.

It is this covenantal tradition, old and new, which will provide the fuel and make it possible to search the biblical map. The stop for fuel and the search will occupy us for the next four chapters.

The pumping of fuel begins with that motley group of slaves in Egypt. The story in the book of Exodus is familiar enough. The slaves were hard pressed. The Egyptians "set taskmasters over them to afflict them with heavy burdens . . ." (Exod. 1:11). Moses is born, hidden in the bulrushes, and adopted by Pharoah's daughter. Brought up in the royal household, he sees the affliction of his people and kills an Egyptian for beating a Hebrew. Forced to flee, Moses retreats to the land of Midian and the house of Jethro. The oppression continues, "And the people of Israel groaned under their bondage, and cried out for help. . . . And God heard their groaning . . . and God knew their condition" (Exod. 2:23-25).

This is the stage for God's work of liberation. On it the Israelites say some new things about God. God is one, not many, a unity of creative meaning and purpose. This is not a God who stands aloof in eternal perfection but one who knows and feels suffering, even the suffering of those at the bottom of the pyramid, so to speak.

This understanding of God is still fresh today. So also the responsiveness of God is still fresh. In the Israelite view God not only hears and knows the suffering of the people, but also responds. Again and again in the Exodus story God takes the initiative in response to suffering. The first response is to Moses. God calls him to leadership, appearing to him in a burning bush.[1] Moses is awestruck and hides his face. God persists in the desire to establish a relationship. God says to Moses:

> I have seen the affliction of my people who are in Egypt, and have heard their cry because of their taskmasters; I know their sufferings, and I have come down to deliver them out of the hand of the Egyptians, and to bring them up out of that land to a good and broad land, a land flowing with milk and honey. . . . Come, I will send you to Pharoah that you may bring forth my people, the sons of Israel, out of Egypt (Exod. 3:7-8, 10).

Moses, unsure and in an almost pleading tone, replies, "Who am I that I should go?" To which God answers, "I will be with you." At first glance this exchange seems straightforward. Moses lacks assurance and God is promising to give it to him. A second look,

however, reveals something deeper. Moses' question, "Who am
I?" can be understood as a question of identity. Moses lacks direction. He is a Hebrew brought up in an Egyptian household
and a murderer in exile. He has few roots and no home, hence
no confidence or direction. The profundity comes in God's
answer, "I will be with you." It is a statement of relationship
which on the surface does not seem appropriate to Moses' question. Yet it is more than appropriate. It is the truth of being
related to God. The writers of the story seem to say, in effect,
that you will know who you are when God is with you, that is,
when you are in relation to God—and this will give you all the
power and direction you will need. The writers turn Moses'
lament of weakness into an affirmation about power in relationships.

Thus in relationship God delivers the Hebrews from Egypt.
They do not accomplish their own liberation. It is not a one-
time deliverance, for in it is the promise that God always responds to the needs of the poor and seeks to deliver them from
the powers that hold them in bondage. This is good news to the
poor, news which is being heard and responded to wherever
injustice occurs.

The Exodus story is not one that stops with liberation. Freedom is only the first step in this story's picture of the relationship
to God. It is followed by the call to election and the establishment of a covenant. Liberation, election, and covenant: these are
the three essentials which delineate the nature of a complete
relationship to God.

The Israelites state the call to election in several places, notably Exod. 5:22–6:9.

> "I will deliver you from their bondage, and I will redeem you
> with an outstretched arm and with great acts of judgment, and
> I will take you for my people, and I will be your God; and you
> shall know that I am the Lord your God who has brought you
> out from under the burdens of the Egyptians" (Exod. 6:6-7).

Election is a troubling notion and an often misunderstood experience. It suggests favoritism and has led to the fanatical ex-
cesses of those who mistake their own egos for God and assume
election means God is on their side. This notion need not lead
to these consequences, for in itself it says something very hum-
bling about the human experience of God.

The mystery that the notion of election seeks to explain is the troubling one of why some people are in bondage to external forces such as economic injustice or to their own psychological processes, while others experience liberation, peace, and unity. Why is this so and why do some for no apparent reason or virtue receive the best life has to offer?

For the Hebrews in Egypt the question came in quite specific form: "Why did God deliver us from slavery in Egypt?" They concluded that God, for no apparent reason of special greatness or worthiness, had elected them. Later writers put it this way:

> For you are a people holy to the Lord your God; the Lord your God has chosen you to be a people for his own possession, out of all the peoples that are on the face of the earth. It was not because you were more in number than any other people that the Lord has set his love upon you and chose you, for you were the fewest of all peoples; but it is because the Lord loves you ... (Deut. 7:6-8).

In other words, God elects because God loves. This is the reason the Israelites could give for their election.

Later on the understanding of election became a problem as one disaster followed another. Jerusalem itself fell and the Israelites once again found themselves in captivity, this time in Babylon. What can election mean when the elect are once again in bondage? One answer comes in the prophetc interpretation of events as God's judgment, another in Israel's understanding of election as servanthood.[2] Israel in the latter view was not elected to greatness and prosperity even though it might experience both at times. Israel was elected to serve God, or to use the imagery of the prophet Hosea, to be a responsive lover.

Today the idea of election is out of favor and discredited by misuse. But the mystery the idea points to is still very much with us. The experience of undeserved freedom, peace, and unity comes in many different forms. Some are very personal. Others, with the exodus of the Hebrews from Egypt, are social. These experiences have a common denominator. They all call us out of self-centeredness and into relations with others.

A good personal analogy to what the Hebrews must have felt is our own deeply meaningful moments of love. Almost all of us can confess to a sense of liberation, peace, and unity in such moments. These moments include the sense of freedom from a fragmented and compulsive preoccupation with the self. This sense of liberation is not just freedom from the self. It is also the freedom in and for the other, and the sense of an emptying yet fulfilling peace which comes from being selflessly in love and from letting the other person's needs and cares take the place of our own. It is also the sense of the unity of two previously separated people and the unity of one's own self which finds its home in a love which transforms brokenness into wholeness.

This freedom, peace, and unity in love is something we often strive for by attempting to apply ever greater amounts of will-power. This is the wrong way, for self-assertion never is successful in producing these moments. There is no way by our own will-power, either by force or seduction, to make another love us, or more importantly, to make us love them. The experience of love is always one of gift, and an undeserved one at that. Rewards are what we have come to expect for achievement. Love, however, while it can be sought, cannot be striven for or achieved; and hence its coming never seems earned or deserved.

So we ask: why are these things so? Why does love come to us in this moment? Why not to someone else in another moment? Why not to the really poor, to the man who has never known an ounce of love, or to the woman who has lived for her entire life abandoned in miserable and degrading poverty? Certainly they have a greater need for it than we do.

The creation stands silent in the face of these mysteries. Some have tried unsuccessfully to reduce mystery to science through psychology and social analysis and others to cover it over with dogmatic assertions. In the last analysis the story the Hebrews told is as good as any. God rescued them from Egypt and elected them to be a servant people. The reason can only be that God loves. It is a story which has stood the test of time and tells what is most essential and significant in a puzzling existence.

Covenant

Covenant follows exodus and election as the third element in the story. Covenant is our response to God's loving act of liberation. In the Hebrew scriptures it is stated in several places. It is often preceded by a recitation of God's mighty acts of deliverance and the words, "now therefore," indicating that what follows is the expected response to the gracious gift.

"You have seen what I did to the Egyptians, and how I bore
you on eagles' wings and brought you to myself. Now therefore, if you will obey my voice and keep my covenant, you
shall be my own possession among all peoples; for all the earth
is mine, and you shall be to me a kingdom of priests and a holy
nation" (Exod. 19:4-6a).

The order is significant. The response does not precede the
gift. The Hebrews in their day and we in ours are not asked to
keep the covenant before we are free to do so. The laws and
rules which come after the "now therefore" are not something
we must do to get to God. It is the other way around. God has
freed us first, has taken the initiative and come to us, and only
then given laws and rules as guidance for what a loving response
on our part might be.

Put differently, being free precedes the doing of the law. We
must be in relationship to God before we are able to do the law.
Both the freedom and the law are gifts. This is important to
remember because the great emphasis placed on law in Hebrew
Scriptures and in certain forms of Christianity sometimes obscures
the dynamics of relationship which undergird it. The law tends
to take center stage and to draw attention away from liberation
and election for service. Whenever this happens the dynamics are
lost, the relationship broken, and a cold, impersonal obligation
substituted. We are wise at such points to turn to the prophet
Micah who sums up the law and in so doing preserves the
quality of freeing gift that leads to relationship.

For I brought you up from the land of Egypt, and redeemed
you from the house of bondage . . . and what does the Lord
require of you but to do justice, and to love kindness, and to
walk humbly with your God? (Mic. 6:4a, 8).

Exodus, election, covenant—these then are the three terms of
the relationship to God in Hebrew Scriptures. They set the pattern for subsequent statements of the relationship to God including the one in Jesus Christ. They set this pattern, not because
there is some intrinsic goodness to following patterns, but because this is the way that God seems to work, that is, by freeing
people for service. Significantly, they set this pattern for a people. There was no concept of the individual among the Hebrews, only the whole, the Chosen People. This is difficult to un-

derstand. Just as we look at technology in terms of distinct inventions, so we see society in terms of individuals. This way of thinking which focuses on parts instead of wholes obscures the dynamics of groups just as it misses the total impact of many technologies acting together. We must retain both the individual and the corporate responses in our efforts to secure fuel and gain direction.

The Prophetic Response

The history of Israel is an object lesson in the difficulty of living the covenant and of staying in relation to God. It is a history filled with those vain imaginings, petty vices, and bloody aggressions which are the stuff of self-centeredness and national pride. The Israelites told stories about an inevitable tendency to fall out of relationships to God, nature, and other persons. It perplexed them that they knew what it meant to be in relationship but could not consistently respond in keeping with their knowledge. These stories are found throughout the Hebrew Scriptures, perhaps most poignantly in the Genesis account of Adam and Eve. That story is familiar enough, but its essence as a statement about pride, self-centeredness, and separation from God, nature, and other persons is often forgotten.

As the calamities which regularly follow pride and separation befell Israel, a group of men came forward, empowered by God and speaking the truth. They were called prophets and had a sense about relationships that enabled them to see into the future. They were able to see into the future not because they possessed powers of clairvoyance, but because they understood the consequences of closed and broken relationships, notably injustice, neglect of the poor, arbitrary and dictatorial leadership, war, and revolution. To the Israelites, the prophets announced that devastating consequences would follow and in so doing recalled Israel to her covenant with God.[3]

They did more than just point to past events. They made clear that relationship to God is an ongoing process. The events which brought liberation, election, and covenant were not relics of history to be mounted in some museum of the mind. The God who acted then acts now and will continue to love Israel and to call for a response guided by the terms of the covenant. The relationship to God is dynamic, not static.

In announcing the calamities which would befall Israel, the

prophets brought to the fore the notion of God's judgment. Judgment is a term that quickly arouses resistance in us. We conjure up pictures of self-righteous moralists threatening doom and gloom in order to produce guilt where there was none before. What the prophets were saying, indeed continue to say, should not be confused with efforts at psychological manipulation.

God's judgment is part of God's love. It is the other side of mercy and forgiveness. It is what we experience when we are not open and are unable to do justice, to love kindness, and to walk humbly with God. Here the crude image of God as a father punishing his errant children obscures more than it illuminates. We need to redo our image in this case. God works through love, and the love we experience in relationship to God, nature, and other persons is a more fitting image or analogy. If God's love and justice are received as liberation and election and responded to with the keeping of the covenant, then the lack of love and justice has its way of being received and responded to also. This is the insight of the prophets. Judgment is part of God's love and justice. It is the absence of God, or, to put it in a way which sounds contradictory but really is not, the awful presence of God. We are still related to God in judgment, but we experience God as absent or against us, as in depression, apathy, broken relations, wars, and rebellions. These negative experiences are the presence of God because they represent God's call back to relationship. It is through judgment that we are made aware of our wrong direction as persons and as a people.

For the prophets, however, judgment was never the last word from God. Judgment is preliminary and preparatory, for beyond God's judgment is mercy and forgiveness. The prophets expressed this element of mercy and forgiveness in terms of the survival of a remnant which would reestablish the covenant in a purified Jerusalem.[4] To the exiles in Babylon in the sixth century before the Christian era the prophet known as Second Isaiah spoke not of the judgment which had befallen the Jews in the destruction of Jerusalem and the deportation, but of a new exodus, a new return to Jerusalem made easy by God leading the way (Isa. 40:1-5).

In other words, beyond our experience of depression, apathy, separation, war, and rebellion, love makes possible the reestablishment of relation both for individuals and groups. Again, it is God who makes this possible.

As the prophets added these new insights of judgment and mercy to the notions of exodus, election, and convenant, they also spelled out more forcefully the basic terms of the covenant. In particular for our purposes, they reiterated God's concern for the poor, which first surfaced in God's hearing the suffering cries of Israel in bondage to Egypt. As Israel's prosperity grew, so did its neglect of the poor, of authentic worship, and of justice. The idolatry of wealth and selfish consumption, the pomp of an imperial monarchy divorced from the needs of the people, and political intrigues had made a mockery of the covenant. Amos put the case forcefully:

> I hate, I despise your feasts,
>   and I take no delight in your solemn assemblies.
> Even though you offer me your burnt offerings and cereal
>   offerings,
>   I will not accept them,
> and the peace offerings of your fatted beasts
>   I will not look upon.
> Take away from me the noise of your songs;
>   to the melody of your harps I will not listen.
> But let justice roll down like waters,
>   and righteousness like an everflowing stream.
>   (Amos 5:21-24)

Israel was a splintered community. Without justice, concern for the poor, and a responsive government, community is impossible. Without community Israel was not a people and could not, therefore, respond to the covenant. Community is essential to our relationship to God.

CHAPTER 6

Jesus, the Community of God, and Faith

Exodus, election, and covenant have rough counterparts in the message of Jesus summarized in Mark 1:15: "The time is fulfilled, and the kingdom of God is at hand; repent, and believe in the gospel." Here the three terms are the kingdom of God, repentance, and belief. Their similarity to the three notions in Exodus suggests an underlying pattern.

The first strand in this pattern is God's gift. For the Hebrews, this gift was liberation from slavery in Egypt. For Jesus' hearers, it was the troublesome declaration of the coming kingdom. The second strand is a call or challenge which must be heard. For the Hebrews, this was hearing the call to election; for Jesus, repentance. The third is the response which the gift and the call create. For the Hebrews this response was the covenant. For Jesus, it consisted of belief. Gift, call, and response; however stated, these are the essentials of relationship, not only to God but also to other human beings and to the rest of creation.

The Community of God

The kingdom of God is a troublesome term. To start with, there is a problem of language. The term *kingdom* no longer communicates the paradoxical nature of power in the gift. Kings use armies, political manipulation, and economic power to gain their ends. Jesus' kingdom has power but not of this kind. In fact, the power of the kingdom has always been considered weakness by human kings. Second, for those concerned with sexist language, *kingdom* is too restrictive a term. Third, the term *community* is available as an appropriate substitute and is a more fitting term, because in a democratic age it better conveys the communal nature of both God's gift and our response. Thus, taking liberties with the Greek original, we will call it the *community of God*.

The community of God in the message of Jesus is also troublesome because nowhere is it given precise definition, or at least not the precise definition our empirical culture demands. The reason for this lack of precision is the symbolic nature of the term. It cannot be identified with any existing community, but rather points beyond all communities to God's activity in our midst, which even the most devoted believer must admit is seldom easy to define. It is like defining the words *hope, love,* and *spirituality*. Words finally cannot encompass the experiences these words point to. But this does not mean the declaration of the community is without content. God's community is present in our communities and Jesus leaves clues to its nature and presence in both his message and his activities. These clues give us a foundation and some guidance.

At the most general level the community of God is an expression of hope in agreement with the Hebrew notion that God hears the suffering of the poor. It points to a future time when the alienation of the present will be transformed into a perfect community of love and justice. For Paul it involved a shift of the ages and offered promise to those who heard the call and judgment to those who rejected it.

Further clues come in Jesus' refusal to assume the trappings of human power at the beginning of his ministry and in the cross at the end. Jesus is not tempted to rely on normal sources of power and, in this refusal, reveals that God's power is fundamentally different. Control of people, land, and resources does not secure a ticket of entry into the community. The nationalistic aspirations of Israel or any other political entity are not fulfilled by it. The community is not a reward for proper beliefs, righteous behavior, or correct worship. Sound engineering will not generate it. Quite simply, the usual ways of accomplishing what we intend have little to do with its initiation and continuing presence.

The tradition is emphatic that God initiates this power. It is a power which comes from outside the self and the communities of selves. It carries a demand with it, but it is a demand unlike other demands. It can be freely accepted or rejected. It does not involve a loss of freedom, but in fact increases freedom. It does not lay on us the heavy burden of trying to be something we are not. It is rather like the demand placed on us by a helpless infant. The "demanding" cry of the infant pulls us away from ourselves. Its power, like that of a magnet, is one of attraction. It pulls from ahead instead of prodding from behind.

Since no human power can create and sustain it, we are left with the single activity of opening ourselves to it, or, as some would have it, allowing it to open us. A good analogy is listening to the "demanding" cry of the infant. The mode initially is one of receiving. We must first hear the sounds from outside. They trigger a response in us if we are open. We enter into the child's world with comfort and warmth. In that world we intuitively know that aggressive forms of power are inappropriate. If we are closed, we remain unmoved and tied to the sataniclike dynamics of self-centeredness and aggressive self-assertion. The infant suffers.

The power of the community is thus a paradoxical form of power. Its beginning and part of its power are in small, unexpected things which surprise us and reverse our expectations. The community is like a seed which grows (Matt. 13:31-32). It is seen in the good Samaritan caring for the man who was ambushed on the road to Jericho (Luke 10:29-37) and in Jesus' washing of the disciples' feet (John 13:1-11). It holds special promise for "small" people, the slaves in Egypt, the poor, and those without status (Luke 1:51-54). Jesus himself was humbly born in a manger in a remote town of a distant province. His destiny was not that of Caesar or even Herod. The accolades he received at the height of his popularity faded into curses as the powerful tried to meet his challenge with aggressive force. On the cross Jesus is nailed up as a common criminal and put in the tomb without the pomp of a worldly king. We can hardly imagine a less conspicuous place or person for God to appear in, unless we have come to see the power in the small and unexpected and to appreciate the freeing power of Christ's resurrection.

Jesus offers still another clue to the community of God in the parable of the foolish maidens (Matt. 25:1-13). The maidens are to be watchful, for while the time and place of the coming community are soon and near, they are not known exactly. In the words of Jesus, the community is "at hand." The problem with the community being "at hand" is that we are still waiting, and watchfulness is not a particularly well-developed human virtue. If Jesus meant soon, why is it taking so long? How are we to account for the delay?

For the earliest Christians this problem was partially solved by making two affirmations: 1) that the community had actually begun in the person and work of Jesus Christ and was being carried on by the Holy Spirit and the church; and 2) that the community was yet to come in its fullness. Here, but yet to come: a tidy answer, but one that hardly solves the problem of delay.

Yet this answer does have its virtues. It fits the split character of our lives which includes both the experiences of renewing power and of alienating sin. It affirms that the community is present with power and that we experience this power even if we do not know it fully. It thus has the added virtue of providing us with a foundational perspective. We hope, because there is a power at work beyond our limited resources. Simultaneously we are realistic and prudent, because this fullness is yet to come and sin persists.

The experience of the present community pushes us to inquire after further clues. In what sort of activities might we expect to find the community? The decisive clue comes in the person of Jesus Christ. God chose a person, a humble carpenter, to be the vehicle of revelation. This suggests one place where the community can be expected, that is, in persons. In Jesus Christ God has chosen to relate personally, not anonymously or impersonally. We may therefore expect to experience the activity of the Holy Spirit in our personal encounters and in our own communities: one person related to Christ, two persons in love, communities of people sharing together as in the church, and biotic communities as they relate to human communities.

This clue combined with the others points us in a direction fundamentally different than that of modern technological society. It points to persons in everyday communities as embodiments of the Holy Spirit and picks up what was said in the preceding chapter about election and covenant. Again, the ap-

propriate analogy is our experience of love. Love, that is, God's
self-giving love in Jesus Christ, is the decisive clue for understanding the community of God. Love is given and received only
in community. Love within community and efforts to engineer
human existence without participation are in deep tension. We
cannot engineer love, and control kills it, for love is a gift and
is possible only when freely assented to. This is why love and
technology seem so far apart in our culture. Psychologist Rollo
May talks about the warfare between love and technology.

> But it is not at all clear that technology and eros are com-
> patible, or even live without perpetual warfare. The lover, like
> the poet, is a menace on the assembly line. Eros breaks exist-
> ing forms and creates new ones and that, naturally, is a threat
> to technology. Technology requires regularity, predictability,
> and runs by the clock. The untamed eros fights against all con-
> cepts and confines of time.[1]

The crux of the matter is power. Just as God's community
has power so love has power. It is the only power that can overcome the separation called sin. It alone gives unity. This power
to give personal unity stands in stark contrast to military, political, and economic power. However important these forms of
power are in human affairs, and however much love calls us to
participate in them, they cannot produce unity in us. They
necessarily involve manipulation and coercion, both in deep
tension with love.

Love within community is found, or rather finds us, in and
through small and seemingly insignificant things. A gesture, a
glance, a touch, a simple congruence—these are the stuff of love
as they are of community. Love also comes in larger sizes, as in
justice among peoples, but for most of us large size overwhelms
and generates impersonal relationships in which it is difficult to
receive love.

Because it often comes in small packages we overlook it. It
passes us by unnoticed as we fix on Rome, Washington, Moscow, or the latest computer game. We have come to expect
power only through normal channels. Thus when love touches
us we often miss it or are surprised to discover we have been
looking for it in the wrong place.

Jesus said that the community is at hand. Reinterpreted in
terms of love, we can say the community is as near as the closest

person or tree. It is also at hand in another sense. It is urgent. Perhaps this is the way Jesus meant the words *at hand* to be understood. Love is indeed urgent. Without it we cannot be unified. We know God only as judge. To be unified, or, to use a much abused theological word, to be *saved,* is a matter of spiritual life and death.

Repentance

This leads to repentance, the second term of Jesus' message. The word *repentance* runs a close second to salvation in terms of abuse. The very mention of the word conjures up stereotypical images of pulpit-thumping preachers manipulating feelings of guilt over petty vices. Repentance is much more fundamental than the rejection of petty vices which the exercise of a little willpower can handle without a change in basic orientation. Repentance in the way Jesus understood it means a change of basic orientation or direction. The change called for is from a basic preoccupation with the self and the things which provide self-security to a basic preoccupation with God's community. In terms of the love analogy, it means putting love and justice first.

How do we repent? What are its dynamics? The key is to see repentance as openness or the will to be open. To repent is to open ourselves to the possibility of God's love. Herein lies an old theological puzzle which we do not need to settle. It has to do with the question of whether we can will to be open to God's love or whether the power of love catches us by surprise and opens us up in spite of ourselves. On some occasions there seems to be a limited capacity to open ourselves to the possibility of love. We make decisions and reach out in a certain direction. On other occasions, for example in moments of despair or depression, freshening new insight seems to pull us up or a little girl whispering something in our ear catches us short.

We do not need to solve this puzzle of grace. We need only point out that repentance is a change of direction from being closed to being open to God's community. It is putting ourselves in a receiving or listening mood or acknowledging the work of grace in us.

The first act of participation in God's community is, therefore, to receive the love which makes community possible. Beyond this, repentance is also a call to activity and engagement in such things as prayer, confession, solidarity with the poor, the appreciation of beauty, and respect for the rest of creation. Of particular importance is the confession of our own part in the structures and values which have led us to the end of the superhighway.

Belief

The third term in Jesus' message is belief. The word *belief* suggests rationality, a statement of basic principles, or a verbal affirmation of faith. These understandings are not incorrect. They are merely partial, for Jesus meant far more in his message about God's community. The intellectual capacity to systemize statements of faith are pointers to a greater essence.

Belief, like covenant in response to liberation, has to do with our response to God's gracious gift of community. We trust in the power of God's community to make us whole. This trust is active, not passive. The unity in love we experience does not allow passivity, at least not for long. It makes us active lovers and seekers after justice. That is its character.

Consider the cross of Jesus Christ and its power in our lives. If we are sensitive and compassionate, that is, open to the suffering of another, we can experience something of Jesus' trial on the cross. Suffering is compelling. It draws us outside of ourselves. Our own sufferings and troubles are trivialized. They seem so unimportant by comparison to the love which would sacrifice a son or daughter and the love which would endure a crucifixion. Participating in his suffering, as in any suffering, has a liberating effect. We commune with Christ and sense we are part of him and no longer centered on ourselves. This participation also gives us unity and direction. We intuitively trust it and desire to become servants. Similarly, in the resurrection we experience the exaltation of Christ's victory over the spiritual death that sin leaves us in. The exaltation is powerful. It forces us to form communities to work for justice and to go out like the apostles to spread the good news.

Belief then is the desire to become a servant; the trust that through the experience of the cross and resurrection we really are in touch with what is essential; and the activity of going out into the world in behalf of this trust, guided by the covenant and the teachings of Jesus. It is in simplest terms our response to the community which is now at work in our midst.

Faith

The gift, the receiving of the gift, and the response—these three things form the dynamic of our relationship to God. Theologian Paul Tillich called this dynamic faith, or the state of being ultimately concerned.[2] Faith, in Tillich's view, involves an act of the total person, including mind, will, and emotion.[3] It presupposes an element of "infinity" in us which enables us to receive power from, and to respond to, the truly ultimate.

According to Tillich there are two sides to the activity of faith, the subjective and the objective.[4] The subjective side is the centered act of our personalities. In Tillich's terms this is the act of having an ultimate concern, in our terms the activity of repentance or openness. The objective side is that to which our acts of openness or expectancy are directed, that is, to use the common symbolic term, God. In the act of faith the subjective-objective split is overcome. God or the ultimate is no longer an object "out there" or the reference of theology, but something within us which provides the unity or belief which overcomes alienation. In greatest intensity it is, according to Tillich, "the feeling of being consumed in the presence of the divine." [5]

Swiss theologian Emil Brunner called this dynamic "truth as encounter."[6] The word *encounter* is appropriate because it fits the analogy of personal interaction which is part of our analysis. Brunner was influenced at this point by Jewish theologian Martin Buber, whose notion of the "I-Thou" relationship is similar to Brunner's language of encounter and ours of gift and response.

Brunner, in his influential book *Truth as Encounter,* set forth several elements of this encounter. The first and most decisive is that the truth about humanity "is not in man, but must come to him." [7] It has come to humanity, according to Brunner, in the person of Jesus Christ, who can only be perceived in an act of faith. The perception of Jesus Christ is that of a God who calls and communicates himself. God's call finds us closed like a lock. God's Word in Jesus forces the lock open, so to speak. It opens the self-enclosed self. This opening is the second element.

The third element is the perception of the encounter as personal. It is not the impersonal truth of theologians, organizations, or technical systems.

> Truth as encounter is not truth about something, not even truth about something mental, about ideas. Rather it is that

truth which breaks in pieces the impersonal concept of truth
and mind, truth that can be adequately expressed only in the
I-Thou form.[8]

The link between the historical revelation in Jesus Christ and
our own encounter with Christ is the fourth element. This link
is love, which is disclosed in Jesus Christ as the meaning of life.
Love also calls forth the activity of love. This is the fifth element.
A person's deepest nature, claims Brunner, consists in "answer-
ability, i.e., in his existence in the Word of the Creator." [9] In
the call and the person's answer an encounter takes place which
transforms the person. It is the religious root from which "grows
the moral act as its natural necessary consequence." [10] In slightly
different terms: "Fellowship with God is present only when the
creature meets God's love with responding love, when the creature knows and appropriates his freely given love." [11] Faith
then, according to Brunner, "is the complete self-giving of man
which is consequent upon having received the unconditional self-
giving of God." [12]

The final element is the perception that truth as encounter
cannot be possessed. "Its nature is . . . such that it takes possession of us, lays hold of us. . . . The truth with which faith is
concerned can only be received." [13]

The Washing of Feet

The Gospel According to John illustrates this dynamic and
the theology of Tillich and Brunner. In John 13:1-11 is found
the well-known story of the servant Jesus washing his disciples'
feet as they prepare for supper on the night of his betrayal.
Amazingly, in this most critical hour it is feet which receive
Jesus' attention. One of the most abused parts of the anatomy
becomes the object of God's love! The event in John's account
speaks for itself. No words are needed. Nor do we need an elaborate theology of the suffering servant to get the message. Peter
represents us all by picking up the topsy-turvy nature of what
Jesus was doing. No doubt he was surprised and did not expect
this sort of reversal. "Lord, do you wash my feet?" (v. 6), Peter
asks. It is the question of one who expects the rookie, not the
veteran, to perform such lowly acts of servanthood. It is the
response of one who still does not see God's gift of community
in the small and apparently weak things of life.

Jesus' response to Peter suggests that something more than mere foot washing is going on here. "What I am doing you do not know now, but afterward you will understand" (v. 7). Here John is referring to the coming events of the cross and resurrection which ultimately will reveal the purpose of Jesus' work. But we should not let such telescoping obscure what is happening in the moment. In the small, seemingly insignificant act of washing feet Jesus hints at the essence of God's power, which is the power of love incarnating itself in human affairs.

Peter, however, misses the obvious, just as we often do. Although he feels the power, he comprehends neither the coming events nor the paradoxical nature of God's love in the moment. He replies to Jesus (v. 8), "You shall never wash my feet," and in so doing refuses the gift of community. Jesus' response confirms this: "If I do not wash you, you have no part in me" (v. 8).

In other words, unless we allow God's love to disarm and open us to the point of receiving love, we do not participate in Christ or the dynamics of faith. To be disarmed or open is to be selfless. To be selfless is to be both a receiving disciple and a responding servant.

Selflessness has many faces. Preeminently it takes the form of suffering for or with someone else. But it is also experienced as forgetfulness of self, as when we play hard and lose sense of time and space, or engage in conversation only to note at the end that the hour passed like 10 minutes. In such events we are truly "outside" ourselves. We are not focused inwardly. We have lost ourselves in the sense of not being consciously aware of ourselves. We might even say we are most ourselves when least ourselves, that is, most whole when we are not focused on ourselves but on others. Indeed, it is not stretching things to say that in deeply loving encounters we die to ourselves, both in the sense of losing consciousness of self and in the sense of the eternity of love.

There is a kind of knowing or belief that goes on in deeply loving encounters. It is not the knowing of empirical proof as in science, but something we may call "participative knowing." It is a way of knowing that motivates action far more intensely than empirical knowledge. Participative knowing or faith comes from the sense of unity and wholeness which love gives to us. We know because we are known (1 Cor. 13:12). This intensity

comes in degrees, from doubtful and tentative responses of care
to more intense forms of mutual sharing. The former are more
common, but the latter usually set the tone for our lives by
providing a deep spiritual foundation and a plumbline which
gives standards for judgment.

To sum up, Jesus reveals God's community as the power of
self-giving love. We experience this love often through small
and apparently weak acts which surprise and disarm us, such
as the washing of feet. What is experienced and revealed to us
through participation is that personal unity and the ability to
respond come when we are drawn out by love and allow ourselves to respond by sharing in the other. We give ourselves
and in so doing get ourselves back in a transformed way, in
Christ. This is faith.

Our illustration must give us pause, however. Something is
missing. This something is pointed to by Argentinian theologian
Jose Miguez Bonino. Miguez Bonino asks the question, "In what
realm of human experience and activity shall we find the categories for naming the themes of theology?" [14] His answer involves a criticism of excessively individualistic categories and
analogies and the use of so-called existential theologies. In
the Latin American context faith must talk about an oppressive
political reality. Washing feet may be appropriate elsewhere,
but God in Jesus Christ also hears the voices of suffering in Latin
America and calls us to respond. Exclusion of the social and political realities threatens to turn our theology into an ideology
of the rich who find it convenient to shift from issues of social
justice to those of personal experience. Consequently we must
add justice to our understanding of faith. The present-day struggle for justice, no less than God's liberation of Israel, the words
of the prophets, and the teaching and example of Jesus, is the
place where God is most certainly working.

The Content of Faith

Our fuel for the way ahead is faith. Christian responses to the
critical issues of the day must have their foundation in the
dynamics of encounter. The failure to recognize this plagues the
efforts of many churches seeking to address these issues. Social
analysis and activity without access to the basic fuel of faith

soon runs out of gas. It loses its spirit and power. Without faith, as without vision, the people perish.

Motive power is not direction, however. Here the fuel analogy breaks down. While faith does give some direction, especially in problems of a highly personal nature, with the social problems of hunger, poverty, pollution, and technology faith is only the first step in directing our responses.

So we must ask, "What is to be our response to God's community already at work?" To answer this question requires more than a willingness to repent and believe. It also means study of Scripture and of the witness of the church for guidelines to go along with our study of the problems in earlier chapters. In other words, our response needs guidance on these problems. Faith is our fuel, but we need a map to find our way through the maze of these problems and to avoid our own tendency to take directions which satisfy our own interests first.

When we combine faith with the sources of guidance available in a process of prayer, reflection, and creative imagination, we have some grounds for expecting a fitting response to God's community. This process is never perfect. Any conclusion must remain tentative and be periodically reevaluated. The community of God is yet to come, not only in its fullness, but in our own deliberations.

PART 3

The Map: Rough and Defined Bearings

CHAPTER 7

Justice and Participation

We are not looking for maps with detailed contours. Exact directions are simply not available. What we need at this point to give content to faith are rough bearings in the form of values and guidelines. Our sources of direction will be Scripture, the witness of the church, our own experience of God's love and justice, and our best thinking about the problems. Our starting point will be the recent witness of ecumenical Christianity, in particular the World Council of Churches' vision of the just, participatory, and sustainable society, and what the National Council of Churches in the United States calls the "ethic of ecological justice." [1]

Central to the World Council's vision and the National Council's ethic are three core values: justice, participation, and sustainable sufficiency.[2] These three values, and 12 guidelines which give them greater specificity, are the subjects of the next two chapters.

Justice

Justice is rooted in the very being of God according to the Christian tradition. It is an essential part of God's community of love and calls us to make fairness the touchstone of our social response to other persons and to the rest of creation. Justice is not the love of Christ *(agapē)*. Justice involves a calculation of rewards and deserts. Justice has a more impersonal quality than love because nations and groups are more its subject than individuals. Nevertheless, justice divorced from love deteriorates into a mere calculation of interests and finally into a cynical balancing of power against power. Without love societies lack the push and pull from their members to move them to greater approximations of justice. Love forces a recognition of the other's needs. Love judges abuses of justice. Love lends passion to justice. Finally, insofar as love is already victorious over sin, it is a powerful force preparing the ground for justice by making us open to the needs and interests of others. Justice, in short, is love worked out in arenas where the needs of each individual are impossible to know.

The biblical basis of justice, with its special sensitivity for the poor, is clear and obvious. It starts with God's liberation of the poor and oppressed slaves in Egypt and the establishment of a covenant, one of whose cardinal features is social justice.

> You shall not wrong a stranger or oppress him, for you were strangers in the land of Egypt. You shall not afflict any widow or orphan. If you do afflict them, and they cry out to me, I will surely hear their cry; and my wrath will burn (Exod. 22:21-24).[3]

The biblical basis continues in the prophetic reinterpretation of the covenant. Critical to their reinterpretation were justice and a concern for the poor and powerless. Micah summarized the law (Mic. 6:8) : "to do justice, and to love kindness, and to walk humbly with your God." Amos was adamant that God's wrath would befall Israel for its transgressions. Important among those transgressions were injustice and the failure to care for the poor. The powerful "sell the righteous for silver and the needy for a pair of shoes" (Amos 2:6), profit by cheating the poor (Amos 8:4-8), and trample the poor (Amos 5:11). Isaiah and Jeremiah were equally adamant.

> Woe to those who decree iniquitous decrees, and the writers who keep writing oppression, to turn aside the needy from justice and to rob the poor of my people of their right, that widows may be their spoil, and that they may make the fatherless their prey! (Isa. 10:1-2).[4]

The story is no different in the New Testament. The emphasis on social justice is somewhat muted by comparison to the prophets, but the concern for the poor may be even stronger.[5] Jesus himself was a poor man from a poor part of Israel. His mission was among the poor. His message was directed to the poor.

> And he came to Nazareth, where he had been brought up; and he went to the synagogue, as his custom was, on the sabbath day. And he stood up to read; and there was given to him the book of the prophet Isaiah. He opened the book and found the place where it was written, "The Spirit of the Lord is upon me, because he has anointed me to preach good news to the poor. He has sent me to proclaim release to the captives and recovering of sight to the blind, to set at liberty those who are oppressed, to proclaim the acceptable year of the Lord." And he closed the book, and gave it back to the attendant, and sat down; and the eyes of all in the synagogue were fixed on him. And he began to say to them, "Today this scripture has been fulfilled in your hearing" (Luke 4:16-21).

He blessed the poor and spoke God's judgment on the rich (Luke 6:20-26 and Matt. 5:1-14). On the cross he made himself one of the dispossessed.

The early church carried this tradition beyond the time of Jesus. Paul's concern is frequently the weak members of the community. This is his concern as he addresses the question of eating meat sacrificed to idols in 1 Corinthians 8. Here he affirms the new freedom in faith which is one important foundation of political freedom. Freedom, however, is not license to ignore or persecute the weak in the pursuit of one's own consumption. Freedom, yes! But true Christian freedom is slavery, that is to say, service to one's neighbor, with particular sensitivity for the weak.

Paul is even more emphatic on equality which, with freedom, is the backbone of the modern concept of justice. His statement of the ideals of freedom and equality in Christ are among the strongest in the entire biblical witness. This fact is in no way diminished by his more conservative interpretations in actual situations where he apparently perceived a need to moderate the rigor of his ideals for the sake of community harmony. Thus, while Paul seems to advise an inferior role for women in the church (1 Cor. 14:34-36) and urges the slave to return to his master (Philemon), his ringing affirmation of equality in Gal. 3:27-28 has through the ages sustained Christians concerned about justice.

> For as many of you were baptized into Christ have put on Christ. There is neither Jew nor Greek, there is neither slave nor free, there is neither male nor female; for you are all one in Christ Jesus.

In the early Jerusalem community, as recorded in Acts 1-5, this radical equality was actually put into practice.[6] The community provided for the economic needs of every person. Members of the community were willing to share all their possessions so that none would be deprived of basic needs. This experiment yielded less than perfect results, but still the fact remains that the immediate followers of Jesus saw radical equality as part of their response. The early Christians at least attempted to establish communities of freedom and equality. In so doing they set themselves apart from the prevailing Roman culture. What set them apart were not the compromises with equality and freedom that are inevitable in any human organization. The difference was what they took to be their guiding principles. Freedom and equality were at the center of their Christian life, not the status quo and its concessions.

In Western philosophical tradition justice means treating equals equally, unequals unequally. Justice is more precisely defined in this tradition by speaking of it in terms of freedom and equality.[7] In part this reflects the influence of the Christian tradition in which these two principles are central. Political liberty is a derivative of Christian freedom and a necessary condition of living in communities of love.[8] Equality stems from an understanding of persons made in the image of God (Genesis 1) and the basic equality of each person in Christ.

Justice defined in terms of freedom and equality is thus a rough bearing derived from our biblical map. Perfect justice would characterize life in the community of God. Unfortunately, the community is yet to come in its fullness. Coercion, inequality, and unfair treatment abound. Humans settle for compromises which depart markedly from the ideal and call them just. In situations where the ideal and reality are far apart, Christians are faced with a dilemma. Should we stick to the ideal or accept compromises which represent only approximations of the ideal?

This question will occupy us in greater detail in forthcoming chapters. For now we assert a presumption in favor of the ideal. The burden of proof is on those who would deny freedoms, increase economic and political inequality, and implement inequitable policies.[9] Departures from freedom and equality are justifiable only on the presentation for public scrutiny of relevant and reasonable grounds for believing that a greater good will be achieved.

Establishing relevancy and reasonableness is notoriously difficult. A quick glance reveals that societies impose coercion, justify inequalities, and enact inequitable policies for a host of relevant and irrelevant reasons. Yet, to reiterate, from the Christian perspective the burden of proof rests on those who would depart from freedom and equality. They must make their case. The bias in Christian ethics is with the ideal and with a special sensitivity to the impact of existing and proposed actions on the poor.

Reasonableness or proportionality is also difficult to assess. The amount of coercion, inequality, and inequity allowed should never exceed the good that it produces. If, for example, the supply of energy for basic needs requires restrictions and unequal distribution of income and wealth, as some claim, tyranny and extremes of affluence and poverty are not thereby justified.

Relevancy and reasonableness are further complicated by the general acceptance of the status quo, which always includes unsupportable coercion and inequality. The status quo, if it has enough time to settle in, becomes the measure of justice and the ideal of freedom and equality. Departures, even if they move a society closer to the ideal, are made to bear the burden of proof, and screams of injustice are heard from the privileged and those who benefit from injustice.

In summary, justice is the social equivalent of love and means special concern for the poor, a rough calculation of freedom and equality, and a passion for fairness. The ethical aim of justice in the absence of other considerations should be to relieve the worst conditions of poverty, powerlessness, and exploitation; to support programs that help the poor and malnourished to achieve productive, useful, and sharing lives; to avoid coercion; and to narrow inequalities. In questions of energy and resources it should be the provision of sufficient and sustainable energy and resources to all and an equitable distribution of burdens and costs among members of each community and between generations. Finally, it is the establishment and maintenance of basic human rights as set forth, for example, in the United Nations Universal Declaration of Human Rights.

Participation

Participation is also implicit in God's community. It has the same threefold pattern as faith, which is its source of power. Gift, openness, and response—participation is dialog between selves and between the self and society and the rest of creation.

Participation is important on two levels. The first level is participation in close personal relationships. Participation on this level is not the focus of this study, but is crucial to it. If personal relationships are poor, the individual is easily swallowed up by society or experiences difficulty with identity and direction. This is especially true in modern industrial society, where impersonal, functional relationships prevail.

Mike Mulligan exemplifies this first level in the best way in his relationship with Mary Anne, his "almost" human steam shovel. The town of Popperville, to which Mike and Mary Anne retire after losing the battle of technologies, is another good example. People have names and characters in Popperville, and decisions are more or less a community product.

The second level of participation is the social level and our principle focus. On this level participation is much more difficult, especially in complex technical societies. A multitude of decisions, each requiring expert technical judgments and having wide-ranging consequences, must be made in a timely way. Popular participation, particularly when there is conflict, can paralyze essential processes.

Popperville represents social participation most of us can handle. Unfortunately, the Poppervilles of the world are being overwhelmed by not-so-distant cities, modern forms of mass communication, and the values associated with modern technology. The way of relating in close, personal fashion fostered in Popperville is in trouble. The impersonal, functional way of relating which consigned Mike and Mary Anne to the junk heap is creeping slowly toward Popperville with its mixture of new freedoms and greater alienations. The danger is that this impersonal and functional way of relating will continue to reduce participation on the social level. The danger goes further, for the two levels of participation are not independent. Impersonal and functional modes easily creep into our personal relationships producing difficulties with love and will. Psychologist Rollo May claims:

> The world presented by our contemporary painters and dramatists and other artists is a schizoid world. They present the condition of our world which makes the tasks of loving and willing peculiarly difficult. It is a world in which, amid all the vastly developed means of communication that bombard us on all sides, actual personal communication is exceedingly difficult and rare. The most significant dramatists of our time . . . are those who take as their subject matter precisely this loss of communication. . . .[10]

For our purposes participation on the social level means, at minimum, having a voice in the critical decisions which affect one's life. For the problems under consideration, this means having a say in the energy and resource systems our society selects, the technologies these systems incorporate, and the type and distribution of benefits and burdens these systems create. It also means a say in the organization and distribution of food production and the guarantee of meaningful employment so far as it is a social possibility.

All this implies free and open elections and a responsive democratic government. These two things go a long way to ensure participation by individuals. On the international level, access by nations to forums where critical decisions are made and openness to the decisions of these forums is also implied.

Participation, needless to say, is not assured by a responsive democratic government. Central to participation and timely decisions is a viable community where mutuality, solidarity, diversity, and spiritual growth are high priorities. For this to happen, the community must have structure and purpose and be limited in its scope. This is the truth of Popperville in modern industrial society. We need to pause and reflect on this because it is so central to all that is being said. Community is the key.

For Christians, community begins in and gets its sustaining power from God, not individuals. This sounds obvious, because it is so deeply ingrained in Christian thought. But the implications of starting with the most encompassing whole we can know are enormous. God in Christ is the center, not individuals. Christians find their center in the whole, not in the parts. The tremendous emphasis on individuals and their freedom to do as they please is not the direction of Christian responses. Rather, the direction of our faithful responses is toward ever greater wholes: from the individual to communities, from communities to nations, from nations to the principle of "common heritage," and eventually to God.

This does not mean a smothering of the individual in impersonal and authoritarian collectives. It does, however, give weight to the common good and to communities. We are members of a body. We need these bodies for our sustenance and nurture. They are the primary locus of God's activity. There is a "common heritage" which can be appealed to, for example, in devising laws of the sea.

This primacy of the whole is implicit in Jesus' announcement of the community of God. The task is to see the relevance of God's community for human communities. To insist on relevance is not to advocate a Christian state or to force religious perspectives where the separation of church and state properly applies. The experience of God's community will not permit these kinds of relevance. What we are looking for in God's community are insights which offer wisdom about human communities.

The place to start is with the characteristics of the community in the teachings of Jesus and with his insistence that God's community has its source in a different kind of power, essentially the power of love and justice. This power and this power alone is capable of producing genuine and satisfying human communities. Acceptance of it at the center of our beings and as the direction for our activities is urgent.

This insistence by Jesus may sound trite. Christians have been saying it for centuries, and its repetition in the face of continuing reliance on traditional forms of power lends an air of unreality. Nonetheless it is true. Genuine human community cannot be engineered. Technologies, material consumption, and economic growth may enhance human power, but they offer little help in developing participative communities or in overcoming the alienation of modern society. Reliance on these powers can only make matters worse, by creating divisions as each country grabs for scarce resources to ensure material security. St. Augustine was correct. It really is at heart a matter of what you love.

Jesus also stressed the beginning of the community in small

things. Here we must be careful. Equating the community of
God with the ideology of "small is beautiful" is not appropriate.[11] Large size is sometimes more efficient, and community can
be found pocketed even in mammoth bureaucracies. Yet we
would do well to think the unexpected, that is, "smaller," especially in an age which thinks "big." Jesus' message suggests we
are overlooking something in our pell-mell rush to increase the
size and complexity of social organization and technological
processes. For an effective community size must be limited in
order for the individual to have significant and satisfying contacts.

This suggestion is confirmed by experience. The things that
make for community are often found in the small and seemingly
insignificant: a caress on the cheek, the washing of feet, and the
small act of kindness in a local church. It is these things that
most often make for community and participation, not the things
which overwhem us with their power and size. Here again the
community of God is telling us something about directions: size
can make a difference.

The community of God in the teachings of Jesus also mandates a concern for the poor. This concern is much more than
philanthropy and alms. It is first and foremost social justice.
What this suggests, and our experience again confirms, is the
centrality of social justice to community. Without some semblance of justice there can be little participation in community
and hence little human wholeness. Extremes of wealth and poverty and disproportions of power create an envious and angry
underclass. Equality of worth, rough equality of power, and
political freedom are prerequisites for genuine communities, be
they God's or ours. Once again the direction is clear. Community calls for justice.

The manifestation of God's community in the early church
confirms these directions. The model taken from Jesus' own ministry, from the early community in Jerusalem (Acts 1–5), and
from Paul's writings (for example, Romans 12, Philippians 2,
and his notion of the church as the body of Christ) all point
to the biblical norm of small, holistic, and participatory communities. Jesus gathered a community largely of the poor and
needy. He gave and found support in a small inner group of disciples who apparently shared things in common. In the book
of Acts we encounter a group where the response to Christ is

spontaneous and voluntary and led to what Ernst Troeltsch called "love communism." In Jerusalem the community was central. Community members offered their possessions as need arose. They were determined to have no one be in want of basics.[12]

While the Pauline communities did not duplicate the Jerusalem community, the norm was in Paul's mind. Romans 12 is perhaps the most ideal statement of what God's community should look like. It echoes the Sermon on the Mount in Matthew 5-7. Its image of the body of Christ with its many members strikes a major theme in Paul's writings, perhaps best seen in 1 Cor. 12:12-30. The church is the body of Christ with many members, all of whom are united in Christ. Differences between Jew and Greek, male and female, slave and free are not important. Notions of superiority are rejected. The goal of the group's activities is to build up the body, to edify, and to strengthen the community.[13]

We know of course that the ideal was never realized in any New Testament community. Moreover, we live in a different time and place. The extended family, small town living, the agrarian nature of traditional life, and the special circumstances of New Testament times are largely things of the past. The need to supply enough food and energy in a timely way to meet the demands of five billion people necessitates efficient and productive social organizations. All of these things reduce the immediate relevance of the examples.

Yet the examples stand. The Bible has authority for Christians as the Word of God. The response of early Christians to God's gift was the formation of small, caring, and participative communities. Indeed, there may even be an inherited human disposition for small, closely knit groups, a disposition handed down over thousands of years when this was the only form of social organization. Big size, centralized and impersonal groupings, and too much stress on the individual violate this heritage as well as the New Testament ideal.

Somehow we must learn to put our large productive organizations with their awesome technologies together with our need for intimate communities. No sure way to do this on a mass scale is now clear. However it is accomplished will require planning and control of technology, but planning and control in themselves will not do the trick. Planning, as Jacques Ellul tells us, is itself a technology or method, and methods never create human wholeness. God, in relationship to people, creates wholeness, and the most important way God carries this out is through participative communities. So the task is to combine planning with a new emphasis on community.

Helpful in this project will be the notion of appropriateness. Coined in relation to a certain style of technology and popularized by the late E. F. Schumacher and Amory Lovins, the concept seeks to conform technology and social organization to the needs of community. The World Council Conference at M.I.T. had this to say about appropriate technology in regard to the transfer of modern technology:

> The alternative to this ill-advised transfer of alien technology is the development of appropriate technology. The word "appropriate" should not be understood as implying some minimal level which will always keep developing countries in a dependent position. Rather, it should represent technology which is in harmony with the needs, culture and environment of a particular society. Certain questions should always be asked in evaluating a particular technology: it is "for whom," "for what" and "by whose decision?" In a political conflict, "by whose decision" becomes the most important and includes the other two questions. If developing countries are to opt for appropriate technologies, they must formulate and enact a coherent system of social goals which serve the interests of the people. The absence of a political system in which people truly participate is the major barrier to this. . . . If appropriate technology is to be developed, the people must share in decisions about goals and means of production. They must be educated and politicized so that they become aware of their social situation, can direct themselves through decision-making, and use their dormant collective power.[14]

CHAPTER 8

Sustainable Sufficiency and Guidelines for Response

Of the three values, sustainable sufficiency is the one having the most to do with the provision of life's basic necessities. As such, it takes a certain priority, for without basic necessities justice and participation are all but impossible. An empty stomach or the prospect of starvation in a world where there is plenty of food are injustices in themselves and make it difficult to participate in anything except grubbing for survival. Once basic necessities are supplied, however, sustainable sufficiency loses its priority and takes its place alongside justice and participation.

The term *sufficiency* has been added to sustainability to reflect something which was implied but not made explicit in World Council discussions. The term *sustainability* alone does not reveal the problem with the timely supply of basic necessities. Sustainability does not automatically mean sufficiency. The two are not always compatible. Bountiful harvests this year, for example, may be bought at the price of soil exhaustion and future crops.

Sufficiency is the timely supply to all persons of basic material necessities defined as the resources needed for food, clothing, shelter, transportation, health care, and some margin above subsistence.[1] The stress is on the words *basic needs* and their definition in terms of things that are genuinely basic. Sufficiency is

not the supply of each and every human want. Luxurious and
wasteful consumption are not part of it. In the words of the
Report from Section VI at the World Council Conference at
M.I.T.:

> Basic needs include material needs of food, shelter, clothing,
> resources, and services, and non-material needs relating to
> human fulfillment, the sense of meaning and the quality of
> community life. Happily the human being is not a machine
> whose needs can be entirely quantified. It is important that
> basic material needs be met in ways appropriate to the non-
> material needs of the whole person. We can speak of a vital
> minimum of biophysical needs necessary for a dignified sur-
> vival. It is important to distinguish also what is needed for
> survival in any society with its specific social and economic
> system and culture. The perception of these needs may change
> with the transformation of the social system. In addition there
> are wants which do not fall in either of the above categories
> and which derive from adopted lifestyles; these are not basic.[2]

This emphasis on basics implies a reduction in consumption by
those consuming in excess of basics and an increase in consumption by those who find themselves short of basics.

Sustainability in turn refers to the long-range capacity of the
earth to supply resources for basic needs at a reasonable cost
to society and the environment. It assumes a limited capacity of
the earth to yield resources and to absorb pollution. It also assumes the fallibility of human technologies and organizations in
dealing with the complexities of natural and social systems.

Sufficiency

The biblical understanding of justice, wealth, consumption,
and sharing are the basis for an understanding of sufficiency. The
basis of sufficiency in justice builds on what has already been
said. In the present world where widespread poverty persists in
the midst of considerable affluence, justice means that the poor
should have first access to resources to the point where basic
needs are supplied. This mandates the transferral of income and
capital to the poor in ways that avoid dependency and promote
self-sufficiency. This mandate calls for a willingness to give, wisdom in the creation of transfer mechanisms, and a determina-
tion to achieve self-sufficiency.

Biblical attitudes toward wealth also inform an understanding of sufficiency. Two general, and not altogether compatible, attitudes dominate biblical writings. On the one side there is a qualified appreciation of wealth, on the other a call to freedom from possessions which sometimes borders on deep suspicion of them.[3] The Hebrew Scriptures take the former side, praising the rich man who is just and placing a high estimate on riches gained through honest work. Alongside this praise is an obligation to care for the weaker members of society.[4] Nowhere do the Hebrew Scriptures praise self-imposed poverty or beggars.

Both sides are found in the teachings of Jesus. The announcement of the coming community of God carries with it a call for unparalleled righteousness, freedom from possessions, and complete trust in God. The service of God and the service of riches are incompatible.[5] Jesus himself had no possessions and prodded his disciples into the renunciation of possessions and sacrificial poverty.[6] He proclaimed good tidings to the poor and liberty to the captives.[7]

Nevertheless, Jesus took for granted the owning of property. He was apparently supported by women of means and urged that possessions be used to help those in need.[8] Jesus did not ask Zacchaeus to give up all his possessions. He dined with hated tax collectors and was fond of celebrations, especially meals of fellowship. These examples move in the Hebrew direction of stressing the right use of wealth.

This mixed mind continued in the early church. On the one side was the Jerusalem community, where goods were shared in common. This seems to follow Jesus' preachings about radical freedom from possessions. On the other side stands Paul, who did not address the problem of wealth although he himself had few possessions and was self-supporting as a tentmaker. He did, however, stress right use and called on his congregations to support the poor in Jerusalem.

The biblical witness on consumption follows much the same pattern. The basic issue in the New Testament and later in the early Christian community was that of self-denial versus contentment with a moderate level of consumption.[9] On the one side were those who translated Jesus' radical teachings about wealth and possessions and his own way of living into a full-blown asceticism. This movement eventually evolved into monasticism. From the beginning of the third century in Egypt we find ascetic monks gathered in communities.

On the other side we have a Jesus who, as was noted, was fond of celebrations and meals of fellowship. Along this line Paul preached an inner freedom which emphasized contentment with self-sufficiency.[10] This is expressed most vividly in a later letter attributed to Paul.

> There is great gain in godliness with contentment; for we brought nothing into the world, and cannot take anything out of the world; but if we have food and clothing, with these we shall be content (1 Tim. 6:6-8).

Among those who preached contentment, ascetic rigor was seldom present. Modest possessions were permissible. Emerging from this in later periods is something German scholar Martin Hengel calls "the compromise of effective compensation."[11] What this compromise amounted to was the justification of wealth and possessions so long as a willingness to give and right use are present.

> For the communities of the second and third centuries with their often well-organized, generous care for the poor and social concern, which called for a constant stream of money and responsible administration of it, the "compromise," which did not reject the rich but laid extra financial demands on them, was the only practical expedient. As a result, possessions acquired a contradictory aspect. They were regarded simultaneously as a dangerous threat and a supreme obligation. . . . Suspicion of riches largely continued in the communities, but abundant giving was nevertheless sought and appreciation of it reflected in part on the giver.[12]

In summary, sufficiency in terms of the timely supply of basic needs is a value derived from several biblical concerns. Justice and its special concern for the poor is one foundation. The side of the tradition which stresses radical discipleship, voluntary poverty, and self-denial points to the satisfaction which is experienced in simple living without possessions. Finally, there is the other side of the tradition which argues for contentment with modest consumption, the right use of possessions, and the duty of the rich to give liberally. From all sides comes the guidance that minimum sufficiency takes precedence over the piling up of possessions.

Sustainability

Sustainability is closely related to sufficiency. Sustainability is the long-range supply of sufficient resources for basic needs. Taken alone, sustainability easily becomes an ideology of the rich, as we have observed on several occasions. Justice calls us first to the supply of basic needs and then to long-range sustainability. The task is to see that sustainability and sufficiency are not at odds and that, once basic needs are satisfied, even higher levels of production are sustainable.[13]

Sustainable sufficiency applies to both human beings and to the rest of creation. The two must be kept together. A one-sided tendency to stress human welfare to the exclusion of the rest of creation is partially responsible for the present concern over limits to growth. This stress cannot continue, for human beings themselves depend on and are part of the rest of creation. Yet to take the other extreme is no solution either. A mindless pro-earth, antigrowth position, like sustainability taken alone, becomes a self-serving ideology. Certainly we can work towards a reasonable harmony with the rest of creation and not abandon our concern for justice.

Sustainable sufficiency is basically good stewardship and is a pressing concern because of human sin. In the Bible stewardship is care for the earth and care for persons.[14] It embodies Edmund Burke's ongoing view of society, in which ancestors and posterity are seen as sharing in the decisions of the present. The present generation takes in trust a gift from the past with the responsibility of passing it on in no worse condition. A concern for posterity is one aspect of love. Our response to the love of God includes responsibility for the material and cultural condition of posterity and, since the introduction of powerful and intrusive technologies, increasingly for the rest of creation. Our neighbor's grandchildren, as well as the birds and flowers of the field, are our neighbors.

This view of stewardship has both Old and New Testament foundations. The writers of Genesis introduced the concept in the very first chapter of the Bible.

> So God created man in his image, in the image of God he created him; male and female he created them. And God blessed them, and God said to them, "Be fruitful and multi-

ply, and fill the earth and subdue it; and have dominion over
the fish of the sea and over the birds of the air and over every
living thing that moves upon the earth."

Two words stand out in this passage: *subdue* and *dominion*. The
Hebrew words are harsh. Elsewhere in the Hebrew Scriptures
they are used in connection with stamping or treading on
grapes.[15] This meaning is inadequate for the context, however.
According to biblical scholar W. Lee Humphries, those words
were addressed to a people forcibly removed to a strange land,
Babylonia. Their God seemed impotent, and their imaginations
were constantly turning to the pantheon of appealing Babylonian
nature gods. In this situation the writers used strong and harsh
words. To the Israelites in exile, the words held promise that
Yahweh the God of Israel was not impotent and that the nature
gods of Babylon were part of the creation and hence under the
rule of Yahweh and even under the dominion of men and women.

Humphries goes on to argue that dominion in Gen. 1:26-28 is
to be understood in terms of stewardship. In the larger view of
the Hebrew Scriptures men and women are seen as God's vice-
roys. It is God who owns the earth as a king. The viceroy has
complete authority as commissioned by the king. In the words of
Humphries, "the viceroy patterns his rule on that of his Lord. . . .
And the king upon whom the viceroy patterns his rule is not a
capricious despot, but the God of sacred history, the God of
promise, of the exodus and deliverance, the God of the covenant."[16] Elsewhere political scientist J. Patrick Dobel comments:

> The world is given to all. Its heritage is something of endur-
> ing value designed to benefit all future generations. Those
> who receive such a gift and benefit from it are duty-bound to
> conserve the resources and pass them on for future genera-
> tions to enjoy.[17]

We must also note that Genesis 1, while written late in the
history of Israel, appears in the text before the fall in Genesis 3.
We hear nothing in Genesis 1 about violence and conflict.[18]
Harmony prevails between humans and the rest of creation. To
have dominion and to subdue within this harmony means something quite different than it does to a mind conditioned by conflict and violence.

The harmony of the Garden of Eden presupposed in Genesis 1

does not last, however, and in the fall human beings become alienated from God and from the rest of creation. In Genesis 3 we have the fall itself. In Genesis 4 fratricide and revenge take hold, and in Genesis 6–9 comes the story of the flood. In Genesis 6:11 we read, "Now the earth was corrupt in God's eyes, and the earth was filled with violence." The flood follows as God's judgment. A new covenant is made, but with the understanding that violence will persist. According to Heidelberg pastor Gerhard Liedke:

> It is no longer the language of solicitous rule, but of war. The possible conflict of Genesis 1 has broken out wholesale and will cease only at the end of the ages when men and beasts live together in harmony as Isaiah 11 foresees. In our world, however, man's dominion is the fundamental form of relation between man and the non-human creation.[19]

In other words, the careful stewardship envisioned in Genesis 1 has turned into the violence of Genesis 3–9 through human sin. The separation of persons from God is the root cause of our present unsustainable patterns of life and of the violence we do to the rest of creation.

This understanding is carried into the New Testament. In Rom. 8:18 the whole creation suffers and in 8:22 it "groans in travail." In fact we are now experiencing unprecedented suffering in the nonhuman creation. But suffering, according to Paul, does not lead to despair. "The creation waits with eager longing for the revealing of the sons of God" (8:19), and "in this hope we were saved" (8:24). Suffering, as in the suffering of Jesus Christ on the cross, points us beyond to the hope which is already partially present. Part of this hope is an end to violence and a return to the good stewardship of Genesis 1. Again according to Gerhard Liedke:

> Certainly . . . Christians do not redeem creation. But the creation looks anxiously and longingly to the Christians. By the way in which Christians deal with suffering, the creation is shown how its hope stands. . . . If we human beings increase the suffering in the world—that of men and of the non-human creation—then the hope of the creation sinks. . . . If on the other hand, in solidarity with the non-human creation we reduce suffering, then the creation's hope of freedom awakens to new life.[20]

This hope for a renewed stewardship is vividly expressed in the Gospels. The shepherd cares for the lost sheep. The earth is a vineyard and we its tenants. The steward is held accountable for his stewardship and the servants for the talents entrusted to them. As in the Hebrew Scriptures, we have been given dominion in trust. We have betrayed that trust and brought suffering to the rest of creation. Nevertheless, we are still responsible to God. We are called to be stewards and to exercise dominion with love, care, and nurture, not destruction, rape, and pillage.

In addition to this view of stewardship, there is an important biblical view which holds that the rest of creation is good independently of human beings. God declared it "very good" (Gen. 1:31). It is not simply here for our use but possesses an autonomous status in the eyes of God. Ultimately, it belongs to God, not to us.

We may even grant a provisional personhood to the rest of creation. The Hebrew writers, while frequently seeing the rest of creation as objective, orderly, and impersonal, also portray it as personal, alive, and subjective.[21] Jewish theologian Martin Buber saw the possibility of active encounter with a tree.[22] Indeed, creation might better be seen as a continuum from inanimate to animate matter. The tendency in our culture is to see discontinuity and to view the rest of creation as something to be used exclusively for human purposes. Perhaps if we viewed the rest of creation as filled with Spirit, we would avoid some of our more devastating intrusions.

Twelve Guidelines

The derivation of rough bearings is now complete. One task remains in our map work. Justice, participation, and sustainable sufficiency are like the rough cardinal points north, east, south, and west. They need refinement for more accurate direction. The task is to refine these general values into usable guidelines.[23] The guidelines are useful, not only in formulating our own responses to hunger and poverty, technology, and limits to growth, but also in the advocacy of appropriate social policy. Each guideline has its own specific relevance, depending on the activity or policy being considered. None of them is relevant to every situation. In some cases guidelines will conflict. In others they may carry different weights. As a result, applying them is not an exact science and must be carried out with some tentativeness.

1. *International order* is the one guideline derived from all three values which points to the potential of an activity or policy to decrease the prospects of armed conflict. Without international order all three values are in jeopardy. Activities and policies should narrow the gap between rich and poor which occasions conflict. They should enhance international cooperation without creating patterns of domination and dependency. Finally they should provide for peaceful alternatives to disputes.

2. *Employment* is derived from justice and participation and concerns the impact of an activity or policy on employment levels, skills, and the meaningfulness of work. Activities and policies should stimulate the creation of meaningful work and new and improved skills.

3. *Fairness* is a derivative of justice and has to do with the equity of activities and policies and their impact on the poor and vulnerable. Benefits and burdens should be assessed and distributed so that no group bears a disproportionate share. The improved economic welfare and increased political power and participation of the poor and vulnerable should be primary considerations. The provision of basic human rights is assumed.

4. *Appropriateness* refers to the tailoring of activities and policies to: a) the production of basic needs, b) human capacities, c) end uses, d) local demand, e) employment levels, and f) cultural practices. It is derived from both participation and sustainable sufficiency. Activities and policies should encourage a variety of scales and end uses which do not require infallible or error-free performances from humans and machines. Activities and policies should contribute to community participation and mutuality and be communicable to nonexperts.

5. *Decision making* points to the need for participation in and timely resolution of necessary decisions. It is not just the value of participation transformed into a guideline. The need for timely decisions also makes it a derivative of sustainable sufficiency. Activities and policies should contain provisions for both participation and resolution of differences by individuals, communities, and nations. Harmonizing such provisions will seldom be

an easy task, especially when sensitivity to minority viewpoints is factored in.

6. *Adequacy* refers to the priority in activities and policies of supplying basic needs worldwide and is derived from the value of sustainable sufficiency. This guideline must be given heavy priority to the point where basic needs are satisfied, whereupon it assumes reduced relative importance. Where basic needs are met, frugality and conservation should govern supply.

7. *Efficiency* is the capability of an activity or policy to produce basic goods and services with the input of less resources. Its source is the value of sustainable sufficiency. Activities and policies should discourage wasteful and unessential consumption and encourage efficiency through better design in production and use, the matching of scale and quality to end use,[24] and the education and employment of persons.

8. *Renewability* is an essential guideline for the application of sustainable sufficiency. It refers to the capacity of an energy or agricultural system to replenish itself. By expanding this guideline to include long-lasting though not necessarily renewable systems, it includes such things as recycling and increased durability. Activities and policies should encourage the use of renewable systems.

9. *Risk* concerns the potential of an activity or policy to cause unacceptable harm to health, social institutions, and specific ecological systems. It is derived primarily from sustainable sufficiency but can also be related to both justice and participation. Policies should encourage low-risk systems and mandate strict environmental and human safeguards in all activities.

10. *Cost* refers to the monetary cost of an activity or policy and is derived primarily from sustainable sufficiency. All costs should be counted, including the costs of avoiding risks. Activities and policies should minimize total costs.

11. *Flexibility* is the capacity of an activity or policy for change. It, too, is primarily derived from sustainable sufficiency. Activities and policies should be reversible within a reasonable amount of time and responsive to new technical innovations. Systems vulnerable to sudden disruption should be avoided.

12. *Aesthetics* points to beauty as one aspect of sustainable sufficiency. Activities and policies can be both sustainable and sufficient in quantitative terms but lack beauty. Activities and policies should enhance or cause minimal damage to the beauty of the human and natural environment.

With these 12 guidelines derived from the three core values we conclude our map study. Before we can proceed, however, we face several forks in the road and must make some decisions. These decisions will be easy for some and agonizing for others. They have to do with commitment and character and stem from an unresolved dilemma that has troubled Christians since biblical times.

PART 4
Negotiating the Forks

CHAPTER 9

Rigor and Responsibility: An Unresolved Dilemma

The task, put off from Chapter 1, is to negotiate three forks in the road at the end of our superhighway assumptions. Each fork forces a choice between alternative routes to the just, participatory, and sustainable society. The alternative routes offer their distinct ways of living and accomplishing the tasks at hand, and each promises to be the easiest and best route. We cannot take all of the routes at once or avoid making choices. The routes are not compatible and the forces and interests at work preserving present ways of living have enough momentum to make the choice for us if we do not act.

Some indication of the preferred routes was given in the initial discussion of forks in Chapter 1. A brief review will reacquaint us with that discussion and begin the process of choice.

At the first fork one branch is clear and well traveled. It is the familiar way of the technological fix and is the route which more or less travels a straight line from where we have been. It calls for the unfettering of the technological process as presently constituted and the overcoming of problems through planning, control, and complex, large-scale technologies.

The other way at the first fork is less traveled and less clear. Its sign reads "The Road of Change." It involves justice for the poor and malnourished, appropriate and participative technologies, and a commitment to sustainable sufficiency.

Because the momentum provided by existing social structures and dominant values is so strong, there is an almost irresistible push along the way of the technological fix. In all probability most individuals and societies will follow this, the road of least resistance. Several things could change this. Nuclear war, a revolt of the world's poor, increasing alienation in technological society, the appearance of limits, or the conscious choice to self-limit could alone or in combination make the other alternative more attractive.

Whatever the likelihood of one or a combination of these happening, Christianity presupposes a limited freedom to change. Given this freedom and the analysis of the preceding chapters, the road of change with all its uncertainties is the one to take. It is a route worth pursuing in its own right; and if enough people take it, they will at least act as a leaven moderating the nonparticipatory features of the technological fix.

This brings us to the second fork, one in which the choice is less momentous but still significant. Here one branch offers reliance on changed technologies and social engineering. Value change is not necessary. It is the technological fix mentality oriented in the new direction of justice, participation, and sustainable sufficiency.

In basic agreement with the goal, the other way at this fork does not place as much reliance on technology and social engineering. While not rejecting this reliance, especially not its emphasis on appropriate forms of technology, this way stresses major changes in values and ways of living. In particular, it calls for a basis in faith and living in accordance with biblically derived values and guidelines. Its essence is both new technologies and value change. Again, the conclusions of the preceding chapters lead us down the second road.

This leads immediately to the third and last fork. For Christians it is a troubling fork because it demands a basic decision on how to live in response to the community of God. The choice can be stated in a number of ways. It was present in the discussion of sufficiency, where two basic attitudes toward wealth, consumption and sharing, were seen to prevail in the early church. One stressed a rigorous response to Jesus' teachings including self-denial, the giving of what one has to the poor, and radical freedom from possessions. The other accented the right use of possessions, and, while agreeing that freedom from possessions is fundamental, emphasized responsibility and willingness to share.

The choice was also implicit in the discussion of justice. How far does one take solidarity with the poor and commitment to social justice? Historically many Christians have identified completely with the poor. Well-known modern examples such as Mother Teresa and Dorothy Day have continued this tradition of radical obedience. At the same time, and not so spectacularly, Christians work in different vocations serving Christ with varying degrees of intensity and frugality.

The choice is a dilemma and worthy of further exploration. The dilemma is seen in the question which ended the first chapter: Is it consistent with the life and work of Jesus Christ to be "reasonably" comfortable and to make use of alienating forms of technology in an age of widespread poverty, malnutrition, advanced materialism, and limits to certain forms of growth? This is a dilemma which faces affluent Christians whether or not they are out to buy food or a yacht.

Put differently, it is the dilemma of the real and the ideal. We have glimpses of the ideal in Jesus Christ and his teachings on the community of God. The community of God is already present with power. Yet, paradoxically, it is still to come in its fullness. Reality is a mixture of powers: human power rightly and wrongly used and God's power of love. God's community stands alongside and often in contradiction to human power, and we must live in a world where perfect choices are seldom presented.

Historical Roots

The one choice we will designate *rigorous discipleship,* while recognizing the other is not without rigor. The other choice we will name *responsible consumption,* without calling the rigorous road irresponsible. While the differences between them are significant, it is possible to accept both options as valid Christian ways of living.

We have briefly seen how the early church responded to this choice. Rigor characterized a significant minority in the church and on some issues commanded a majority. Side by side stood an ethic of responsibility which focused on the right use of possessions and radical sharing.

From these two positions a dual ethic emerged. For the monk
or nun who surrendered his or her possessions and elected a life
of chastity, holy poverty, and nonviolence, the rigorous demands
of Jesus were binding. For the rest, the requirements of Christianity were binding, but the more rigorous demands, as in the
Sermon on the Mount, became "counsels of perfection." They
were deemed impossible of fulfillment by all Christians and
therefore binding only on those who would be perfect (Matt.
19:21).

These two ways of living existed side by side, with the authority of the church sanctioning both and holding them together.
Implicit in this resolution of the dilemma was a troublesome
hierarchy of perfection and the unbiblical notion of special merits which practicing the rigorous demands was claimed to confer.
Thus while this ethic resolved the dilemma, it did so at the price
of grading perfection and discouraging the moral effort of ordinary Christians.

Protestants, following Martin Luther's dictum of the priest-
hood of all believers, eliminated special merit at the price of
recreating the dilemma. Monasteries and convents closed and
all believers were, according to Luther, to serve God in whatever
vocation they found themselves. Where there had been two ways
of life in one church, now there was one way with many variations in two churches. The road of rigorous discipleship was not
abandoned, however. It persisted in the monastic movement
within the Roman Catholic Church and in small groups in the
Protestant state churches. It was also vigorously pursued by the
many sects which grew in the fertile soil of the Reformation.

Theological Roots

Theologically the two roads take their cues from the paradoxical "here, but yet to come" teaching of the community of
God. This paradox or tension appears in the earliest pages of
the Bible. Persons are created in the image of God (Genesis 1)
but with Adam fall into sin (Genesis 3). It reappears again and
again in the history of Israel as the Israelites wrestled with the
obligations of the covenant and compared their own weak responses to God's demands in the law. This was particularly true
of the prophets who in their own time represented the more
rigorous side of the tradition.

In the New Testament Jesus advises his disciples to be sheep among the wolves and to have the wisdom of the serpent and the innocence of the dove (Matt. 10:16). For Christians this tension is preeminently present in the cross and resurrection. The cross is reality at its worst and points to the depth of human sin. It points as well to the limitations of individuals and groups and to the need for order and even coercion to keep sin in bounds. It convincingly teaches that living in times short of the community of God involves dealing with the realities of sin and death.

Yet the cross is not the last word in Christianity. It is followed and superseded by the ever-new word of the resurrection. The resurrection points to a God at work in the human situation overcoming sin and death. It points as well to the possibility of "new creations" in the lives of individuals and groups and to the creative potential of love and justice. It teaches Christians that, while they still live in the age of sin and death, God's love has broken in, there is hope, and their efforts in response to God's love are not in vain. Christians are invited as a result to deal with a partly open future where even small responses can make a difference.

The cross and resurrection are tied closely together. Separated they yield a distorted message. The cross alone leads to cynicism, apathy, and resignation to fate. The resurrection alone tends to produce a theology of glory or to degenerate into sentimental illusion or fanatical aggression. The cross and resurrection together teach Christians to be realistic and hopeful and to have the wisdom of the serpent and the innocence of the dove.

Finally, the tension is highlighted by Paul's sense that Christians live between the ages. They live in the old age of sin, death, injustice, and limits. Yet they are called to live according to the new age, inaugurated by Jesus Christ and made present by the Holy Spirit. Insofar as they live in the old age, they give limited support to such things as prison systems, to less than perfect but still functioning economic and political systems, and, even in very rare instances of obvious evil, to wars of liberation and defense. Living in the old age involves compromises, many of which appear to be cop-outs to those who take the rigorous path.

Nevertheless, Christians are not to be serpents or to live according to the old age. They are to live in the resurrection according to the love and justice of the new age. This means

pushing beyond what merely is and the seeking of just, participatory, and sustainable societies. It also means changes in our
superhighway assumptions and the way we live.

Rigorous Discipleship

The theology of the path of rigorous discipleship is easier to
understand and is especially appealing to those with strong
ethical sensitivities. Its advocates are frequently more vocal and
intense. Basically, the position builds on Jesus' call to radical
discipleship, his living without possessions frugally and simply,
and his freedom from material things. In some cases the "love
communism" of early churches is stressed along with a preference for asceticism and self-denial.

Simply put, the Christian is to live a life of simplicity, to
satisfy only the most basic needs, and to give all that he or she
has to the poor. It is a life of surrender to the community of
God. And even if the ethics of the community, as found for example in the Sermon on the Mount, cannot be lived perfectly,
at least the disciple of Jesus should aim in that direction. Living
in the grace of God through faith, the Christian has resources to
respond with total commitment.

As for living between the ages, the path of rigorous discipleship emphasizes the new age almost to the exclusion of the old.
This exclusion comes not from failure to see the sin of the old
age, but rather from the frequent assumption that Christians are
free from the old age through the power of God. Hence radical
changes in ways of living are demanded, and followers make these
changes with enthusiasm.

The path of rigorous discipleship is attractive. It is also validly
Christian. It does not bog down in the inevitable relativities of
the old age. It is simple, direct, and often accompanied by
communities approximating the "love communism" of early
Christianity.

The path is also problematic. Beyond the obvious difficulty of
works righteousness, the wisdom of the serpent suggests ways in
which the old age garbs itself in the disguise of the new age.
The disguises are many. First, many who take this path are predisposed to it by a preference for more ascetic ways of life.
Since most predispositions are the end product of a complex

social process, it should come as no surprise that many elect this path for other than reasons of faith. Some who make claims for the path of rigorous discipleship are not always careful to distinguish their own predispositions from the Word of God. As a consequence their pleas for radical change are heard not as calls to discipleship but as ego-trips.

More subtle is the underestimation of the resilience of the old age. There are, for example, consequences to changed patterns of living in an economy based in the short range on high consumption. One is unemployment, which results from reduced consumption and always strikes the poor first. Related to this is the not easily alterable fact that the means of sustenance for the vast majority is within the existing system. New jobs, new housing, and new transportation systems in the short range are simply not an option except for a minority. Calls to radical obedience need to be carefully tempered with compassion to avoid disabling and dysfunctional guilt. Such guilt is inevitable when perfection is demanded of someone who is trapped in a job which does not fit the standards of the rigorous disciple.

Finally, there is the disguise exposed by critics from the Third World such as C. T. Kurien. When argued by Christians from the developed countries, proposals for sustainability and simple living have the odor of a new program to keep the poor in their misery. The poor of the world are already living sustainably. What they need to survive is more, not less, material things. Calls to changed ways of living must therefore be carefully directed and include provisions for justice and redistribution.

Responsible Consumption

Unlike the path of rigorous discipleship, the path of responsible consumption does not take its main cues directly from the teachings of Jesus Christ. This does not mean it is less biblical, but that it rests more heavily on the main themes of the Bible, in particular on the theological tension between the old and the new ages. Like those on the path of rigorous discipleship, Christians on this path are concerned for the poor and aware of the problem of being tied to possessions. They do not, however, take the asceticism of Jesus literally or urge the surrender of all possessions.

Reduced to basics, those who follow this path wrestle with what it means to live between the ages, taking both ages seriously. In contrast to the heavy stress on the new age, they point to the realities of the old age or to the ambiguity of life between the ages. The problem for them is not radical discipleship but how to act responsibly and to begin a process of change which will lead to sustainable consumption and greater justice. Their mood is sober, their programs moderate and reformist in nature. They also have a greater appreciation of material consumption.

Their path is attractive to less ascetic Christians and admittedly to those who find themselves heavily committed to consumptive ways of living. It is a valid Christian path with several advantages. It avoids the temptation of appeals to feelings of guilt. It accounts for the complexities of living in the world as it is. It does not seek an impossible ideal and thus avoids the illusions and fanaticisms that sometimes accompany appeals to exciting visions of the future. Finally, it offers a Christian response to those who are not predisposed to asceticism.

The position is not without difficulties. A heavy stress on complexity, realism, and limitations has a way of dulling the blade of social change. Complexity easily degenerates into apathy, realism into cynicism, and limitations into conservation of the status quo. Maintaining some semblance of balance between the ages is like picking one's way along a narrow, unmarked mountain ridge. The balance is easily lost, and unfortunately there is a greater tendency with this position to fall into the valley of the old age. The wolf in sheep's clothing appears in this position as selfishness in the skins of responsibility. Finally, the legitimation of consumption can lead to the ratification of selfishness and to the neglect of the poor.

Whither?

Rigorous discipleship and responsible consumption represent two patterns of Christian living. Stated in extreme form they offer a radical choice and are opposed to each other. While stating the positions in this way highlights their distinctiveness, it also exaggerates their oppositions and results in stereotyping. This exaggeration and stereotyping, when coupled with the obvious fact that no one lives either position in the extreme, forces us to step back. The positions need not be seen in opposition.

In the first place, most of us live somewhere between rigor and responsibility. On some issues we are rigorous, on others we lay back either for reasons of energy or interest. On the issues which attract our rigorous attention we may even take differing approaches. In matters of consumption, for example, we may choose simplified ways of living, while at the same time we urge economic growth for the relieving of poverty or admit that simplified living is not to everyone's taste. Or we may take a position that stands between rigor and responsibility. We may elect to simplify but not to the point of bare sufficiency. We may choose to conserve energy without taking every possible step to do so. In short, individuals are not stereotypes.

Second, it is important to keep the two together. It was the genius of the Roman Catholic Church that it could do this for such a long time. It was helped, of course, by a hierarchical and authoritarian social system. It also paid the price of sanctifying different grades of Christian life. Nevertheless, it did recognize that Jesus Christ calls forth from Christians differing responses, each of which may be valid in its own right. The importance of keeping them together also stems from the dialog which ensues. The two patterns can be mutually corrective and help to avoid the worst aspects of each.

Third, the two patterns have several things in common. They both put trust where trust belongs, that is, in God's community in Jesus Christ, not in material possessions or ways of life. Both seek to avoid a self-centered individualism and to be concerned with the affairs of the community, including the distribution of political power. Both are sensitive to the plight of the poor and malnourished and the impacts of social programs on them. Both give limited support to and seek a greater approximation of justice in existing structures. Both agree on the three core values of justice, participation, and sustainable sufficiency.

We may conclude that either of the two forks is a valid Christian route and that Christians should be taking both of them. Perhaps the best analogy is not two roads forking away from each other. Rather, we should see the situation as two lanes on one road with both lanes heading side by side in the same direction. The core of the matter is not that Christians have different patterns of thinking and doing, but that these patterns be kept in dialog. Both ways have their center in Jesus Christ and the church. When that center is lost, the people who take different roads drift apart. They lose sight of their basic agreement on the three core values and concentrate on their differing approaches. This is tragic and unnecessary.

CHAPTER 10

A Response

How then do we respond both to God's community and to the three problems of poverty and malnutrition, modern technology, and limits to growth? So far our mode of response has been the statement of an ethic for the just, participatory, and sustainable society. We began with a study of the three problems. We then turned to the Bible for a religious foundation, finding it in the dynamics of gift, openness, and response. Our next task was to work out a means of relating these dynamics to the problems. For this purpose we developed three ecumenically and biblically based values—justice, participation, and sustainable sufficiency— and 12 guidelines. In the preceding chapter we considered two basic Christian ways of living: rigorous discipleship and responsible consumption, concluding that both were appropriately Christian. Our final task is to indicate our preference for one of these ways of living and to suggest some directions for social policy, the churches, and individuals.

The choice between rigorous discipleship and responsible consumption involves a basic theological judgment. There are many dimensions to this judgment, but perhaps the most important concerns the human situation and the possibilities opened by God's incarnation in Jesus Christ. Does the Word become flesh to provide resources for living rigorously, or, more modestly, for living at all in the midst of alienation? Which are we to stress, the community of God among us or that aspect of the community which is yet to come? Using traditional language, which are we to weigh more heavily, sanctification or justification?

The 20th century has been a time for the reassertion of the relative stress on justification and its underlying premise, the radical disjunction between the sinfulness of human beings and the grace of God. As the century wears on there has been no compelling reason to shift this stress except to avoid its unfortunate tendency toward quietism and to encourage oppressed groups in their struggles for justice. Sanctification still has its place in the development of character, in the recognition of certain exemplary individuals and communities, and in its moral seriousness. The rigorous path remains the way for specially graced and ethically sensitive individuals living in close communities. For the most of us, however, the problem is not sanctification or rigor, but finding the resources to start up. How is one to see the light shining in our darkness? How are we to hear the Word in the noisy silence of Auschwitz, Hiroshima, and the threat of nuclear holocaust? In the words of the psalmist, "How shall we sing the Lord's song in a foreign land?" (Ps. 137:4) The problem is not perfection or discipleship, but finding possibilities. The immediate task is not total transformation, but beginning a process of change.

The way of responsible consumption is more adequate at this point. It emphasizes possibility and change without losing sight of sin and limits. It allows us to hope and have a passion for justice without losing the realization that society is held together more by coercion and power than by morality.

This choice leads us to a certain modesty in making suggestions for social policy, the churches, and individuals. The just, participatory, and sustainable society pursued along the path of responsible consumption is not some panacea leading to the community of God. It may not even take us forward to the highway of ample sufficiency. But it does offer possibilities. It is a way of singing the Lord's song in a strange land of hunger and malnutrition, impersonal technology, and the threat of limits. It is an appropriate way of responding to God's community.

Social Policy

The general goal of the just, participatory, and sustainable society is reasonably clear. It is the timely provision of sufficient and sustainable resources equitably and participatively delivered. In setting our sights on this goal the first priority is not total and immediate transformation, but beginning the process of change. What demands our attention is the transition, the process of moving from superhighway to just, participatory, and sustainable assumptions and actions.

The transition is a matter of great urgency calling for decisiveness. It is particularly urgent for North Americans. We have put the greatest demand on resources and more than anyone else have developed impersonal technological systems. We produce the greatest amount of food and have had the greatest impact on less-developed countries. North Americans will not by themselves solve the problems of hunger and poverty, technological drift, or limits to growth, but they will have a major impact.

The goal of providing sufficient and sustainable resources equitably delivered leads first to *several general recommendations*. The first concerns the timing of the transition and the role of government. The options are to let market forces accomplish the transition in their own good time and way or to make a conscious choice to interfere in the market to accelerate the transition and to ensure justice and participation. There are well-known advantages and disadvantages to each option. On the one hand, market solutions, while relatively efficient, tend to shortchange factors which cannot be stated in monetary terms. In addition, they are frequently slow, unpredictable, and unfair to the poor. On the other hand, the conscious choice to interfere could result in cumbersome bureaucratic manipulations which might accomplish little while spending a lot.

The two options are not mutually exclusive. Market forces should be used when possible to encourage efficiency. To ensure fairness and participation and to speed up the transition, however, conscious social choices should be made and implemented. The government is the only institution so constituted to accomplish this and must therefore assume an active, not a lassiez-faire, role.

The second general recommendation has to do with the 12

guidelines established in Chapter 9. These guidelines should serve as critical and constructive standards for the formulation and implementation of social policy. No policy, of course, can satisfy all the guidelines. A conscious effort to weigh and trade the guidelines off against each other will probably yield better policy. The presence of ethical, political, and economic guidelines on the list encourages a dialog between competing interests.

The third general recommendation concerns resource policy, especially farmlands, minerals, and energy. The values of sustainability and participation push us to a policy of conservation and increased reliance on renewable sources of energy. Implied in this is a restraint of total energy demand, the encouragement of farm practices which preserve the soil, the decreased consumption of depletable energy resources, and the strict enforcement of environmental safeguards. Also implied, and given further push by the value of justice, is the gradual transfer of capital and depletable energy resources to poor countries for the purpose of developing self-sufficient agricultural practices.

The fourth recommendation gives priority to the basic needs of the world's poor. This is the one place where the market system needs more direction than that provided by consumer choices. The poor simply do not have the money to enter the market, hence it can only reflect their preferences inadequately. How the basic needs of the poor are to be met makes a difference. Outright grants to individuals create dependency. The provision of jobs through investment, aid, and trade is preferable so long as it does not create a new dependency. Graduated income and inheritance taxes offer other options.

The fifth and final general recommendation is not a recommendation per se. It concerns communities. Strengthening the family, enhancing individual participation in local communities, and encouraging the peaceful association of communities, especially on the international level, are imperatives. The pressure of our present ways of living on the family, religious institutions, and local communities has continued to reduce their effectiveness as centers of humanization.

The process of decline in these institutions essential to personal integration will probably arrest itself only with significant shifts in priorities and values. Changes in social structure, while important, are probably not sufficient to overcome the economic forces at work. Simplistic formulas and calls to return to the old days are of little help. They ignore the roots of the problem in the dominant position of economic and political institutions in our society and the profound impact of modern technology on values and beliefs. But understanding these roots does not help much, for no way is yet clear to reduce the dominance of political and economic institutions. We are left for the present with Band-Aid measures which help us to care for the sick but do not get at the cause of their disease. Ad hoc organizations formed to offer basic personal support are no substitute for the family or tribe.

On the international level we encounter a similar difficulty. A willingness to participate in international forums and an openness to abide by their resolutions, coupled with the preparation of nonmilitary alternatives to conflict resolution, are crucial. Everyone agrees that these things are crucial but no one knows how to accomplish them. Once again, the problem is relating the whole to the sum of the parts, a problem whose seriousness has increased with the introduction of powerful new technologies. In the nuclear age, however, there is no other alternative to peaceful resolution of conflicts. Realism and national self-interest dictate cooperation because the consequence of non-cooperation is extinction. In this regard, the law of the sea is an excellent example of cooperation and should be ratified by the United States.

Turning to the specific area of *poverty and malnutrition,* we observed in Chapter 2 that the most important cause of high birth rates and poor nutrition was lack of economic security. The innovative work on a small scale of certain Christian agencies is especially important in providing models which might be expanded with the availability of greater resources. The work of these agencies is commendable and should receive the mission support of all churches. For all the good they do, however, they are not sufficient for the larger work of improving overall economic security.

This work, where successful, has begun with a conscious commitment to social justice and the agricultural sector. The title of Frances Moore Lappe and Joseph Collins' book, *Food First,* is apt. The agricultural sector must have first priority. In each developing country this involves the elimination of policies which serve only a wealthy few and the setting of priorities so that self-sufficient food production in fact does come first.

For developed countries this means restraint and a new commitment. Peasant-based initiatives and the reorientation of policy to serve the interests of the poor are seldom inspired by Moscow, however easily so-called Marxists play on discontents. Our reaction of sending arms to the enemies of these initiatives and reorientations, as for example in Latin America, is shortsighted and unrealistic. Rather, we should offer encouragement by letting them be and by helping them to develop their agricultural sectors. This sounds easy to do, but of course runs into the age-old problem of power. We have it and, however enlightened, exercise it in our self-interest. The moral question is whether we can see our self-interest in larger terms and begin to think in ways other than short-term advantage.

Within the food first commitment is agrarian reform, including land redistribution and the provision of supporting services. Aid policies which are geared to reform and the development of self-sufficient agriculture and which are monitored for their effect on farmer incentives are of particular importance. Included under the heading of aid policies is trade liberalization—if not that proposed under the plan of the New International Economic Order, then some plan cooperatively developed and granting temporary advantages to less developed countries.

Further recommendations for social policy are to be found in the Report of Section V of the World Council conference at M.I.T. where member churches were called on:

    i) To foster and give priority to sustainable agriculture in both developed and developing nations, and to strive for policies of land use and management which give maximum sustainable yields without depleting soil fertility;

    ii) To encourage storage of crops at local levels for the sake of self-sufficiency and to counteract excessive profiteering; since in developing countries the greatest loss occurs in the larger storage centers, the most effective preservation and maintenance techniques should be enforced;

    iii) To examine the sustainability of mixed farming versus monoculture;

    iv) To acknowledge the value of indigenous technologies; when technology is transferred three considerations are of critical importance: the appropriateness has to be determined by the recipient; it should be "grafted" upon the

indigenous technology wherever possible; the relationship of the imported technology should be compatible
with the local ecosystem;

v) In the face of diminishing natural resources and energy
supplies, to promote research on the ways of adapting agriculture to these limitations;

vi) To promote reappraisal of land ownership and the priority given to investment in agriculture development;
such a reappraisal will often entail reordering entire political, economic, and social systems;

vii) To set as a primary goal of local and national agriculture policies self-sufficiency in food production, as far as
possible;

viii) To encourage each country to have forestry programs to
regulate the amount of land use for forests, and urgently
introduce reforestation where necessary to ensure soil conservation and water regulation;

ix) To call a halt to the destructive exploitation of the tropical forest.[1]

Shifting to the area of *technology and participation* we find
that making recommendations is much more difficult because
the problems are so little understood and even less appreciated.
It is as if we were standing with Mike Mulligan and Mary Anne
peering down into the junk heap of obsolete steam shovels not
quite comprehending the forces we have named *drift, the technological imperative, reverse adaptation,* and *the whole and the
sum of its parts.* Unlike the general problem of scarcity which
underlies the other problem areas and has constantly been present in the evolution of the human race, the problems associated
with the bloom of modern technology are unique to recent times.
Powerful forces have been unleashed and they have produced
spectacular but ambiguous results.

The harnessing of these forces for humanization and participation is our objective. One proposal which comes immediately
to mind is to put strict controls on technological innovations
and to manage them according to rational goals. Unfortunately,
this proposal presupposes a degree of mastery and control which
we do not possess. We do not now master and control our innovations to the degree commonly assumed, and it is unlikely we
will in the near future. This is not all. As we repeatedly have
pointed out, mastery and control are themselves part of the
problem. They are part of a mind-set which seeks to overcome,

beat back, and subdue. Faith points us in other directions: to openness, to receiving, to the appreciation of the rest of creation, and to letting things be. Finally, the strict control of technological innovations probably would stifle the creative processes from which they flow. This would be no gain for human beings or the rest of creation.

What then are we left with? For one thing, recognition of the problem provides some relief on the individual level. Each of us has limited freedom to begin looking in the nooks and crannies of modern society for the places where genuine communities function. We can be open to the small and surprising events which produce human wholeness. The essence here is repentance, openness, and a change of basic orientation which directs our attention to a new object.

Second, as individuals and groups we should take a more protective posture. Such a posture would include strict environmental laws and zoning practices, and a bias in human communities toward smaller, less complex, less energy-intensive, and renewable technologies. In both of these areas the government has the role of stimulating research and development and enacting adequate protective laws.

Third, a number of tools such as cost/benefit analysis and technological assessment are available. These methods are helpful in calculating the effects of new technologies before their implementation. We have not discussed these tools largely because their effective use depends on the values and beliefs of those who do the analysis or assessment. This does not mean these tools are useless, only that they must be recognized for what they are, that is, techniques. They are only as effective as the people applying them.

Fourth, a commitment to the arts, to the humanities, and to other nonempirical modes of thought is essential. If there is any chance of arresting or at least channeling technological drift and reverse adaptation, it will probably come from a balancing of power against power. The power of religious, broadly humanistic, and artistic modes is considerable, although not of the same type as technical power. The power of these modes lies in their unique capacity to stimulate human integration and creativity. The modern technological process tends to overwhelm and smother them. These modes will never die, but for now they are badly in need of support.

One critical source of support is the church, another the academy. This does not mean pouring huge amounts of new money into ecclesiastical and educational institutions. At this time our society is neither prepared for a reassertion of these modes, nor are these modes stimulated by pecuniary interest beyond a certain minimal level. Rather it means maintaining the basic level of support which now exists and insisting that arts and humanities be included in major educational and social initiatives.

Our final set of recommendations for social policy concerns *sustainable sufficiency*. As we have seen, sufficiency is the timely supply of basic material necessities now and through the transition. It has more of a present focus in comparison to sustainability, which is future oriented and refers to the long-range capacity of the earth to supply sufficient resources for basic needs. Sufficiency takes precedence over sustainability to the point that basic needs are supplied. This precedence is a basic part of justice and must be kept in the forefront of policy in the transition. It should not, however, become the basis for justifying each and every environmentally unsound practice. The timely supply of sufficient resources is not a blank check for profit seekers. The burden of proof for the relaxation of environmental and human safeguards and for the introduction of new technologies rests with those who claim sufficiency is threatened.

Beyond this we should stress the 12 guidelines. They are particularly suited to questions of energy, the environment, and the use of land. For example, a comparison of the various energy alternatives using the guidelines leads social policy in the direction of conservation and renewable resources and away from fossil fuels and sources of energy which utilize large-scale, centralized technologies.[2]

The government has a role to play in leading a social policy commitment to accelerate the period of the transition to sustainable sufficiency. Programs and laws to decrease pollution and waste, energy demand, and the consumption of depletable resources; to increase efficiency in the use of resources; and to expand the practical application of appropriate technologies based on renewable resources are key elements in this social commitment. Quite likely a national investment policy will be required.

Conservation, appropriate solar technologies, and other renewable energy systems should have priority for public funds.

The government is not the only social institution with responsibility for these priorities. Industry, education, churches, and families all must strive to increase social investment in conservation and the efficient use of resources which increase employment opportunities.

Education is a necessary component in the social commitment to accelerate the transition. Again, all social institutions are responsible for educating the public about resource systems; their ownership and control; their social, political, and environmental impacts; and the technical and social policy alternatives available. Because of our heavy dependency on foreign sources of oil, this educational process should include elements which make provision for just and peaceful solutions to sudden disruptions in energy supplies.

Governments, utilities, and energy suppliers should take steps to assure access of the poor to sufficient energy at affordable prices. Special utility rates, energy stamps, and expanded and affordable mass transportation are a few of the available mechanisms. Provisions for the rationing of scarce supplies should be in place for use in emergencies.

To reduce the poverty and malnutrition of the world's poor, significantly increased levels of private and public development assistance are a high priority. This assistance should incorporate the guidelines of appropriateness and participative decision making and be selectively targeted to meet the basic human needs of poor nations and the poor within all nations.

The dilemmas posed by a commitment to energy from nuclear fission and fusion are substantial.[3] On the one hand, the provision of basic needs, the availability of long-lasting supplies, and the unattractiveness of coal make nuclear systems difficult to rule out. On the other hand, there are a number of factors which combine to make nuclear energy incongruent with the ethic of ecological justice. Among these are the risks, real and perceived, associated with nuclear power; the cost of making it reasonably safe and environmentally sound; the effects it has on future social institutions and values; the tying up of large amounts of capital; and the constant threat of weapons proliferation. In addition a highly charged political context makes participatory decision making and timely resolution of disputes almost impossible.

At present there is a de facto moratorium on orders for new

conventional reactors in the United States. Whether this will
continue depends in part on the inexpensive resolution of outstanding problems and the overcoming of political opposition
by proponents of conventional reactors. Should this moratorium
be lifted and new orders lead to the expansion of conventional
nuclear energy, construction should be constrained by strict
environmental and human safeguards. Conventional nuclear
energy should also be seen as a source of last resort, with the
burden of proof resting on the demonstration of a threat to
energy sufficiency. The ultimate goal should be reduced dependence on conventional nuclear energy, with eventual phaseout
as conservation and renewable sources are developed.

The same logic applies to the breeder reactor, only more
strictly. The breeder reactor produces plutonium in far greater
amounts, thereby increasing the waste hazard and the threat of
nuclear proliferation.

With fusion energy the risks, so far as we can know them in
advance, will be reduced, although the impact of complex technologies on society will remain. Fusion offers a potentially huge
source of energy. Research into the feasibility of fusion energy
should therefore continue, but with a careful assessment of social
and environmental impacts.

The recommendation to phase out nuclear fission reinforces
the commitment to conservation and renewable energy sources.
It might also lead to a decision to burn more coal. Coal should
not be seen as some sort of panacea. It is a messy fuel which can
be made acceptably clean only with the expenditure of large
sums. Its expanded use may be necessary to ensure sufficiency,
but such an expansion should come only as the last step before
turning to nuclear energy and only with the protection of strict
environmental and human safeguards.

Finally, and of greatest importance, efforts should be concentrated on *nuclear disarmament*. The avoidance of nuclear war
is a presupposition of justice, participation, and sustainable sufficiency. The weapons position of the United States is more than
sufficient as a credible deterrent. The time is ripe for unilateral
initiatives to reduce arms.

Church Responsibility

The churches no longer dominate society and culture as they
once did. Yet they retain a degree of influence on social policy

and the ways their members live. Responses to God's gift of community are made alive in human communities where prayer, study, and action are the center of community life. The life of the congregation is critical to discernment. God is at work in congregations calling Christians to serve by speaking and doing the truth they discern.

The time is ripe for new life. The ethic of ecological justice and the vision of the just, participatory, and sustainable society offer imaginative ways of thinking which go beyond a mentality of merely staying afloat. The appearance of limits, the poverty of present communities, and the task of responding to the world's poor should be seen by the churches as opportunities, not impositions.

The churches have many ministries in the present situation. First, there is the ministry of education of which this volume is a part. The mission in this ministry is to develop and communicate theological and ethical foundations for justice, participation, and sustainable sufficiency and to support groups within and outside the churches who are experimenting with new ways of living and alternative energy sources.

The second is a ministry of example. The living of justice, participation, and sustainable sufficiency must coincide with the thinking that is their foundation. Conservation and use of renewable energy sources in church buildings, participative and sharing communities, and cooperation in local, national, and international efforts to implement the ethic of ecological justice are just a few marks which will signal movement through the transition.

The third ministry concerns the stewardship of money. In Chapter 2 several church organizations were cited for creative work in less developed countries. In addition, there are secular and other religious organizations already engaged in implementing the new ethic. The churches do not need to set up new organizations. Support of existing groups avoids an unnecessary duplication of effort.

Solidarity with the poor, the malnourished, and the victims of technological obsolescence is the fourth ministry. With continuing high birth rates, rising resource prices, and the quick pace of technological change, the task of standing with the poor, of helping to open channels to them, and of picking up the pieces of broken lives becomes increasingly important.

The fifth and final task is the prophetic one. The mission is to initiate, support, and advocate changes in policy and behavior consistent with the three core values and the 12 guidelines derived from them.

Personal Responsibility

Personal responses of Christians should follow the routes of rigorous discipleship and responsible consumption. As was pointed out at the end of the preceding chapter, these routes have several things in common. They both put trust where trust belongs. Both seek to avoid self-centered individualism and to be concerned with community. Both are sensitive to the plight of the poor. Both have a passion for justice.

For those on the road of rigorous discipleship there are additional responses. Occupations are available which relate directly to the three core values; for example, missionary work with the poor, organic farming, and jobs in the solar-power industry. A preference for simple living with appropriate technologies and the rejection of complex, energy-intensive technologies is an option many have elected. Communal living, or at least participation in close-knit communities, is a frequent pattern. In a few cases all possessions are renounced and basic needs become the norm. In short, rigorous discipleship calls for a radical change in ways of living and stands in stark contrast to the superhighway assumptions which currently dominate.

The route of responsible consumption also involves additional responses. The patterns on this route are less definite. One fairly obvious response is a willingness to share. For example, some have elected to set aside funds to match major purchases in excess of basic needs. So when a television set is purchased, an equal amount is contributed to the church or to an organization working with the poor.

Another response is to conserve energy and resources and to avoid or cut down on unnecessary consumption. Combining several trips into one, buying more energy efficient products with less environmental impact, eating less of certain foods, and careful monitoring of dependency on such technologies as television are all examples of reduced consumption.

Still another is the active support of efforts to conserve resources, to preserve the environment, to seek tax and welfare justice, and to improve the situation of the world's poor. Progressive taxation, self-help programs for the poor, agrarian reform, and low interest loans for home insulation are just a few possibilities.

Finally, those who take this route should and often do work within their churches and other groups to bring about a consistency between activities and the ethic of ecological justice. Given the individualistic bias of American life, this responsibility within groups takes on added importance.

What responsibility finally means cannot, of course, be determined by patterns. There is a situational element to all responsibility which foreswears rigid adherence to prescribed ways. That is why the vision of the just, participatory, and sustainable society can never be a blueprint. Responsibility means sensitivity and requires the openness and responsiveness of faith. Changing situations bring different sensitivities and responses, and the task becomes one of discernment and perception. Who we are and how we stand in faith ultimately are the most important determiners of what we should do.

NOTES

Chapter 1

1. The reports from these conferences are to be found in several issues of *Anticipation,* an occasional magazine put out by the Council's section on Church and Society. See especially issue numbers 18-26 available from Church and Society, 150 Route de Ferney, 1211 Geneva 20, Switzerland.

2. World Council of Churches, "Report: Science and Technology for Human Development," *Anticipation,* No. 19 (November 1974), p. 12.

3. World Council of Churches, "Burning Issues," *Anticipation,* No. 25 (January 1979), pp. 69-73; "Equations for the Future," *Anticipation,* No. 26 (June 1979), pp. 25-31; and Paul Abrecht, ed., *Faith, Science, and the Future,* World Council of Churches, 1978.

4. See, for example: Herman E. Daly, ed., *Toward a Steady-State Economy* (San Francisco: W. H. Freeman and Company, 1973); Amory B. Lovins, *Soft Energy Paths* (Cambridge, Mass.: Ballinger Publishing Company, 1977); William Ophuls, *Ecology and the Politics of Scarcity* (San Francisco: W. H. Freeman and Company, 1977); Dennis Clark Pirages, ed., *The Sustainable Society* (New York: Praeger Publishers, 1977); and Robert L. Stivers, *The Sustainable Society* (Philadelphia: Westminster Press, 1976).

5. Frances Moore Lappé and Joseph Collins, *Food First* (Boston: Houghton Mifflin Company, 1977), Section V.

6. Amory Lovins, *Soft Energy Paths,* Chapter 2.

7. E. F. Schumacher, *Small Is Beautiful: A Study of Economics As If People Mattered* (New York: Harper and Row Publishers, Inc., 1974), Part I, Chapters 2, 4, and 5, and Part II, Chapter 5. In the report of Section VII of the 1979 Conference at M.I.T. six criteria of appropriateness were cited: "i) one criterion for appropriate technology is that the unit of human cooperative effort should not be larger than needed to reach the desired goal without loss of effort, energy and time; ii) appropriate technology should make available products and services which enrich the whole society; iii) it should avoid the waste of material resources through the unnecessary destruction of natural systems and their related carrying capacity (e.g., by recycling materials and reducing pollution); iv) it should use energy as judiciously as possible and consider its availability, if not its ultimate base, as a scarce resource; v) it should have a positive impact on work productivity and welfare distribution among people and among nations by incorporating the work of as many people as feasible; vi) appropriate technology should be conceived and implemented with due regard to the given or desired social context. Report of Section VII: "Restructuring the Industrial and Urban Environment," in *Faith and Science in an Unjust World,* Vol. 2, Paul Abrecht, ed., World Council of Churches, 1980, p. 113. In the Report of Section IX, eleven criteria of appropriateness are cited for the transfer of technology into Third World contexts. See pp. 138f.

8. C. T. Kurien, "Economics of the Just and Sustainable Society: A Third World Perspective," in *Faith and Science in an Unjust World,* ed. Roger L. Shinn, (World Council of Churches, 1980), vol. 1, pp. 220-224.

9. *Ibid.*

10. Report of Section VIII, "Economics of a Just, Participatory, and Sustainable Society," in *Faith and Science in an Unjust World,* ed. Paul Abrecht, vol. 2, pp. 125-134.

11. Jacques Ellul, "Search for an Image," in *Images of the Future,* ed. Robert Bundy (Buffalo, N.Y.: Prometheus Books, 1976), pp. 26f.

12. Elise Boulding, "Religion, Futurism, and Models of Social Change," *Images of the Future,* pp. 169-181.

13. Paul Abrecht, ed., *Faith, Science, and the Future,* pp. 6f.

14. Bruce C. Birch and Larry L. Rasmussen, *The Predicament of the Prosperous,* (Philadelphia: Westminster Press, 1978).

Chapter 2

1. The Presbyterian Church, U.S., and the United Presbyterian Church, U.S.A., *Report to Presbyterians from Washington*, vol. 4, No. 3 (September 1982), p. 1. These statistics are taken from Census Bureau reports.

2. Food and Agricultural Organization of the United Nations (FAO), *Review and Analysis of Agrarian Reform and Rural Development in the Developing Countries Since the Mid-1960s*, 1979, p. 5f.

3. Susan George, *How the Other Half Dies* (Totowa, N.J.: Allanheld, Osmun & Co., 1977), p. 11.

4. Frances Moore Lappé and Joseph Collins, *Food First* (Boston: Houghton Mifflin Company, 1976), p. 13.

5. Radha Sinha, *Food and Poverty* (New York: Holmes and Meier Publishers, 1976), p. 5.

6. Lappé and Collins, *Food First*, p. 66.

7. Barbara Ward, *Progress for a Small Planet* (New York: W. W. Norton & Company, 1979), p. 181.

8. FAO, *Review and Analysis*, p. 36.

9. Lappé and Collins, *Food First*, pp. 13-16.

10. *Ibid*, p. 30.

11. George, *How the Other Half Dies*, p. 36.

12. Lappé and Collins, *Food First*, pp. 131f.

13. George, *How the Other Half Dies*, p. xviii.

14. Lappé and Collins, *Food First*, pp. 76-90, 135-137, 170, 201f.

15. FAO, *Review and Analysis*, pp. 21-39; Sinha, *Food and Poverty*, Chap. 5.

16. FAO, *Review and Analysis*, p. 21.

17. Sinha, *Food and Poverty*, Chap. 6.

18. D. Gale Johnson, *World Food Problems and Prospects* (American Enterprise Institute for Public Policy Research, Washington, D.C., 1975), Chap. 4.

19. FAO, *Review and Analysis*, p. 117.

20. *Ibid.*, p. 110.

21. Sinha, *Food and Poverty*, Chap. 9.; U.S. Department of Commerce, *Statistical Abstract*, 102nd Edition, 1981, p. 841.

22. Presidential Commission on World Hunger, *Preliminary Report*

of the Presidential Commission on World Hunger, Washington, D.C., 1979, I.6; Douglas Ensminger and Paul Bomani, Conquest of World Hunger and Poverty (Ames, Iowa: The Iowa State University Press, 1980), p. 28.

23. William E. Colby, "Food Stamps for International Neighbors," Worldview (January/February 1978), pp. 26-29.

24. Robert L. Rothstein, Global Bargaining (Princeton: Princeton University Press, 1979); United Nations General Assembly, Sixth Special Session, April 19-May 2, 1974, "Declaration of the Establishment of a New International Economic Order," United Nations, 1974; Gamani Corea, "North-South Dialogue at the United Nations," International Affairs, 53, no. 2 (April 1977), pp. 177-201.

25. Arthur Simon, Bread for the World (Grand Rapids: Paulist Press and Wm. B. Eerdmans Publishing Co., 1975), p. 57.

26. Working Committee on Church and Society, World Council of Churches, "Commentary of the Working Committee: Theology, Science, and Human Purpose," Anticipation, No. 25, (January, 1979), p. 72.

Chapter 3

1. Virginia Lee Burton, Mike Mulligan and His Steam Shovel (Boston: Houghton Mifflin Co., 1939).

2. Working Committee on Church and Society, World Council of Churches, "Commentary of the Working Committee: Theology, Science, and Human Purpose," Anticipation, No. 25 (January 1979), p. 72.

3. Schubert Ogden, Faith and Freedom (Nashville: Abingdon Press, 1979), p. 90.

4. The New Delhi Report: The Third Assembly of the World Council of Churches, W. A. Visser 't Hooft, ed. (New York: Association Press, 1962), p. 106.

5. Report of Section IX, "Science/Technology, Political Power and a More Just World Order," Faith and Science in an Unjust World, ed., Paul Abrecht (The World Council of Churches, 1980), vol. 2, p. 138f.

6. Lynn White, Jr., "The Historical Roots of Our Ecological Crisis," Science, vol. 155, no. 3767 (March 10, 1967), pp. 1203-1207; R. H. Tawney, Religion and the Rise of Capitalism (Mentor Books, 1954); Jacques Ellul, The Technological Society, trans. John Wilkinson (New York: Vintage Books, Inc., 1964), pp 32-60; Cyril Richardson,

"A Christian Approach to Ecology," *Religion in Life,* vol. 41, no. 4 (Winter 1972), pp. 462-479.

7. Max Weber, *The Protestant Ethic and the Spirit of Capitalism* (New York: Charles Scribner's Sons, 1904, 1958).

8. Langdon Winner, *Autonomous Technology* (Cambridge, Mass.: The M.I.T. Press, 1977), p. 25. Winner's book is one of the most thorough available on theories about modern technology.

9. This perspective is associated, of course, with the name of Karl Marx. It is not necessary to subscribe to the deterministic elements of Marx's dialectrical materialism to appreciate the influence economic and technological organizations have on values and beliefs, especially in our time.

10. Winner, *Autonomous Technology,* p. 88ff.

11. *Ibid.,* p. 89.

12. *Ibid.,* p. 101f.

13. John Kenneth Galbraith, *The New Industrial State* (New York: The New American Library, 1967), Chap. 2.

14. Winner, *Autonomous Technology,* p. 178ff.

15. Ellul, *The Technological Society,* especially Chap. 2 and pp. 193-227.

16. Siegfried Giedion, *Mechanization Takes Command* (New York: W. W. Norton & Company, Inc., 1969), p. 712.

17. Winner, *Autonomous Technology,* p. 229.

18. *Ibid.,* p. 234.

Chapter 4

1. The generally accepted definition of economic growth is the increase of an economy's output of goods and services over a period of time. It is usually measured by an accounting device known as the gross national product (GNP). In broader, less precise terms economic growth includes the wide range of ideological and material factors that have produced the affluence and abundance of the industrialized countries.

Technology is the application of scientific knowledge to practical problems of producing goods and services. Technological growth is the increase both in scientific knowledge and its utilization to solve problems. More precisely, technology is a process whereby increases occur in the units of output produced per unit of input. Technological growth in this sense means increasing productivity or efficiency and is frequently measured in terms of increasing GNP per man-hour. In its broadest sense technological growth is what Jacques Ellul calls the increase of "technique," that is, "the totality of methods rationally arrived at and having absolute efficiency in every field of human society," (*The Technological Society,* p. xxv). In this usage technological growth expresses the seemingly inevitable increase in rational planning and control characteristic of most industrialized countries.

For further discussion and bibliography see my book, *The Sustainable Society* (Philadelphia: The Westminster Press, 1976).

2. Herman E. Daly, "The Ecological and Moral Necessity for Limiting Economic Growth," *Faith and Science in an Unjust World,* ed., Roger Shinn, vol. 1, p. 215.

3. Kenneth E. Boulding, "The Anxieties of Uncertainty in the Energy Problem," *Prospects for Growth,* ed. Kenneth D. Wilson (New York: Praeger Publishers, 1977), p. 120.

4. Richard H. Wagner, *Environment and Man,* third ed. (New York: W. W. Norton & Company, Inc., 1971, 1978), p. 526.

5. Lester C. Thurow, *The Zero Sum Society* (New York: Basic Books, 1980), p. 107ff.

6. Barry Commoner, *The Closing Circle* (New York: Alfred A. Knopf, 1971), p. 143.

7. *Ibid.,* p. 177.

8. Department of Economic and Social Affairs, *World Energy Supplies: 1950-1974,* United Nations, 1976. Also, Dennis Hayes, *Rays of Hope* (New York: W. W. Norton & Company, Inc., 1977), p. 25.

9. Amory Lovins, *Soft Energy Paths* (Cambridge, Mass.: Ballinger Publishing Company, 1977), p. 33.

10. Robert Stobaugh and Daniel Yergin, "Conclusion: Toward a Balanced Energy Program," *Energy Future,* Robert Stobaugh and Daniel Yergin, eds. (Random House, 1979), p. 216.

11. Presbyterian Church in the U.S. and the United Presbyterian Church in the U.S.A., *The Power to Speak Truth to Power: A Public Policy Statement on Energy, Its Production and Use,* (Office of the General Assembly, 1981), p. 5.

12. Donella H. Meadows, *et. al., The Limits to Growth* (New York: Universe Books, 1972), p. 56f.

13. Daly, *Faith and Science in an Unjust World,* vol. 1, p. 212f.

14. Edison Electric Institute, *Economic Growth for the Future: The Economic Growth Debate in National and Global Perspective* (New York: McGraw Hill, 1976), p. 63.

15. Daniel Bell, "Are There 'Social Limits' to Growth?" *Prospects for Growth,* ed. Kenneth D. Wilson (New York: Praeger Publishers, 1977), p. 21.

16. Commoner, *The Closing Circle,* Chap. 9.

17. Eugene S. Schwartz, *Overkill* (New York: Ballantine Books, 1971).

18. Bell, *Prospects for Growth,* p. 22.

19. Stivers, *The Sustainable Society,* Chaps. 4-6.

20. *Ibid.,* Chaps. 1, 2; Anthony J. Wiener, "Some Functions of Attitudes Toward Economic Growth," *Prospects for Growth,* ed. Kenneth D. Wilson (New York: Praeger Publishers, 1977), p. 53f.; Dennis Clark Pirages, ed., *The Sustainable Society* (New York: Praeger Publishers, 1977), see especially Chap. 8 by Michael E. Kraft; *The Power to Speak Truth to Power,* the Presbyterian Churches, pp. 3, 8, 9.

21. Meadows, *et al., Limits to Growth,* Chap. 3.

22. Robert L. Heilbroner, *An Inquiry into the Human Prospect* (New York: W. W. Norton & Company, Inc., 1974).

23. Barbara Ward, *Progress for a Small Planet* (New York: W. W. Norton & Company, Inc., 1979).

Chapter 5

1. While the story is being told here as if it is literal, I understand this language to be metaphorical and symbolic. All words about God are human words, even those in the Bible. The work of God in the Bible is not the words, the stories, or the images themselves, but the work of love which inspires them. That the ancient Israelites spoke in terms of a burning bush to describe an intense religious experience was appropriate for them. We should not be overly concerned by literalism here. What is important is the affirmation that God was somehow at work with Moses.

2. Exod. 19:16; Isa. 42:6; 53.

3. Isa. 3:13-15; Jer. 5; Amos 2; 5:21-24; 6:1-8.

4. Isa. 1:9; 11:11; 16:14; Amos 9:9-15; Ezek. 9:8; Jer. 44:28.

Chapter 6

1. Rollo May, *Love and Will* (New York: W. W. Norton & Company, Inc., 1969), p. 96.

2. Paul Tillich, *Dynamic of Faith* (New York: Harper & Row Publishers, 1957), p. 1.

3. *Ibid.*, p. 4.

4. *Ibid.*, pp. 9, 10.

5. *Ibid.*, p. 13 .

6. Emil Brunner, *Truth as Encounter*, trans. David Cairns (Philadelphia: The Westminster Press, 1938, 1943, 1964).

7. *Ibid.*, p. 18.

8. *Ibid.*, p. 24.

9. *Ibid.*, p. 19.

10. *Ibid.*, p. 27.

11. *Ibid.*, p. 100.

12. *Ibid.*, p. 104.

13. *Ibid.*, p. 28.

14. Jose Miguez Bonino, *Doing Theology in a Revolutionary Situation* (Philadelphia: Fortress Press, 1975), p. 78.

Chapter 7

1. Division of Church and Society, The National Council of Churches, *Energy and Ethics* (National Council of Churches, 1979). Also see: Presbyterian Church in the U.S. and United Presbyterian Church in the U.S.A., *The Power to Speak Truth to Power: A Public Policy Statement on Energy, Its Production and use* (Office of the General Assembly, 1981).

2. The World Council of Churches uses justice, participation, and sustainability; the National Council, fairness, participation, and sustainability; and the Presbyterians, justice, participation, and sustainable sufficiency.

3. Exod. 22:21f. Also see Exod. 22:25; 23:3, 6, 10-11; Deut. 14:28-29; 15:7-11; 16:9-15; 24:14-18; 26:12-15; Lev. 19:9-10, 15, 33f.; 25:35-38.

4. Isa. 10:1-2; Jer. 22:13-17; Prov. 14:21, 31; 19:17; 21:13; 22:9; 29:7, 14; 31:9, 31:20; Pss. 40:17; 74:19; 86:1; 109:22; Job 33.

5. See Richard Batey, *Jesus and the Poor* (New York: Harper & Row Publishers, 1972); Martin Hengel, *Property and Riches in the Early Church*, trans. John Bowden (Philadelphia: Fortress Press, 1974); J. L. Houlden, *Ethics and the New Testament* (New York: Oxford University Press, 1977), especially Chap. 3; Jack A. Nelson, *Hunger for Justice* (Maryknoll, N.Y.: Orbis Books, 1980); and Walter Pilgrim, *Good News to the Poor* (Minneapolis: Augsburg, 1981).

6. Martin Hengel, *Property and Riches,* Chap. 4.

7. For a more complete analysis see Robert L. Stivers, *The Sustainable Society* (Philadelphia: Westminster Press, 1976) and "Poverty Distribution, and Christian Ethics," in *The American Poor,* ed. John A. Schiller (Minneapolis: Augsburg Publishing House, 1982).

8. Shubert Ogden, *Faith and Freedom* (Nashville: Abingdon Press, 1979). See footnote 4, Chap. 3.

9. Philip A. Wogaman, *A Christian Method of Moral Judgment* (Philadelphia: Westminster Press, 1976), Chap. 2.

10. Rollo May, *Love and Will* (New York: W. W. Norton & Company, Inc., 1969), p. 22.

11. The late British economist E. F. Schumacher introduced the concept in his book, *Small Is Beautiful* (New York: Harper & Row, Publishers, 1973). Since then something of a cult has arisen around the concept. Schumacher was always careful not to let himself be a member of this cult.

12. Martin Hengel, *Property and Riches,* pp. 31ff.

13. Peter Richardson, *Paul's Ethic of Freedom* (Philadelphia: The Westminster Press, 1979), p. 116.

14. Report of Section IX, "Science/Technology, Political Power and a More Just World Order," *Faith and Science in an Unjust World,* ed. Paul Abrecht (World Council of Churches, 1980), vol. 2, p. 139f.

Chapter 8

1. Report of Section VI, "Energy for the Future," *Faith and Science in an Unjust World,* ed. Paul Abrecht (World Council of Churches, 1980), vol 2, p. 93. Also see the Report of Section V, p. 70.

2. *Ibid.*

3. Martin Hengel, *Property and Riches in the Early Church* (Philadelphia: Fortress Press, 1974), especially Chaps. 2, 3, and 9; Richard Batey, *Jesus and the Poor* (New York: Harper & Row, Publishers, 1972), especially Chap. 2; and Walter Pilgrim, *Good News to the Poor* (Minneapolis: Augsburg Publishing House, 1981), especially Chaps. 4, 5, and 6.

4. Amos 8:48; Isa. 5:8-10; 10:1-3.

5. Matt. 6:24; Mark 8:36; 9:43-48; 10:17-25; Luke 12:15; 8:14; 18:18-23; 19:1-10.

6. Matt. 8:20; Mark 1:16; 6:8f.; Luke 9:3; 10:4.

7. Luke 4:16ff.; 7:22.

8. Luke 6:30; 8:2f.; 10:38f.

9. Martin Hengel, *Property and Riches,* Chaps. 7 and 8.

10. Phil. 4:11f.

11. Martin Hengel, *Property and Riches,* Chap. 9.

12. *Ibid.,* p. 69.

13. Report of Section X, "Towards a New Christian Social Ethic and New Social Policies for the Churches," *Faith and Science in an Unjust World,* vol. 2, p. 159f.

14. The biblical understanding of stewardship is the most adequate basis for sustainability. It avoids the tendency in some formulations to escape into nature and deny transcendence. It is in keeping with the traditional notions of human beings as made in the image of God and nature as desacralized. It conforms to the obvious fact that human beings do indeed have a limited control over nature. Finally, it is easily understood.

    This is not to say that other conceptual approaches should be abandoned. In particular, process theology seems to have real potential. Nor is it to ignore several problems with the concept of stewardship. Process theologian John Cobb has criticized the use of stewardship as a concept and norm. "Whereas it suggests that man is an outsider; instead, man is a part of that for which he is concerned and responsible. Whereas it suggests that man brings adequate knowledge with him to his task and can control what occurs; instead he must learn from the world for which he cares how to serve and work with it." John Cobb, *Is It Too Late?* (Bruce, 1972), p. 124.

    To Cobb's critique we may add the problem that the concept of stewardship maintains the dichotomy of superior-inferior and may be too close to the notion of dominion as compulsive manipulation to exert enough of a counter-thrust. The steward as sinner too easily slips from stewardship to exploitation. Thus, if the present crisis is as serious as some critics believe, what may be necessary is a conceptual approach that presents a more radical alternative. This, however, is not my position, although I appreciate the problem that is raised. To accept stewardship as a conceptual approach means to be aware of these problems and to counteract them where possible.

15. W. Lee Humphries, "Pitfalls and Promises of Biblical Texts," *A New Ethic for a New Earth,* ed. Glenn C. Stone (New York: Friendship Press, 1971), p. 101. See for example, Mic. 7:19; Isa. 14:2, 6; Neh. 9:28; Jer. 34:11.

16. *Ibid.,* p. 114.

17. J. Patrick Dobel, "Stewards of the Earth's Resources: A Christian Response to Ecology," *The Christian Century,* vol. 94, no. 32 (October 12, 1977), p. 907.

18. Gerhard Liedke, "Solidarity in Conflict," *Faith and Science in an Unjust World,* ed. Roger Shinn (World Council of Churches, 1980), vol. 1, p. 75.

19. *Ibid.,* p. 77.

20. *Ibid.,* p. 74.

21. Job 31:38-40; Exod. 23:10-11; Lev. 25:1ff., Ps. 96:11f.

22. Martin Buber, *I and Thou,* ed. Ronald Gregor Smith, 2nd ed. (New York: Charles Scribner's Sons, 1958), pp. 7f.

23. In slightly different form these 12 guidelines appear in the joint energy policy statement of the Presbyterian Church in the U.S. and the United Presbyterian Church in the U.S.A., *The Power to Speak Truth to Power,* p. 5. They were developed by a task force for which I was the principle writer.

24. Amory B. Lovins, *Soft Energy Paths* (Cambridge, Mass.: Ballinger Publishing Company, 1977), p. 38ff.

Chapter 10

1. Report of Section V, "Technology, Resources, Environment and Population," *Faith and Science in an Unjust World,* ed. Paul Abrecht (World Council of Churches 1980), vol. 2, p. 75.

2. Presbyterian Church in the U.S. and The United Presbyterian Church in the U.S.A., *The Power to Speak Truth to Power: A Public Policy Statement on Energy, Its Production and Use* (Office of the General Assembly, 1981), pp. 12-14.

3. *Ibid.,* p. 14.

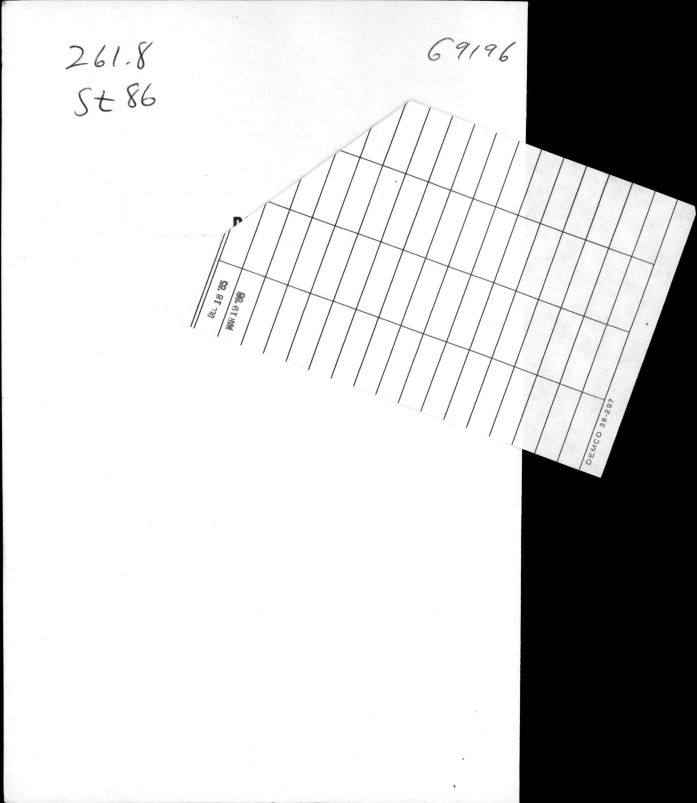